Tarot: Book of Layouts

Volume **1**
Revision: 8/29/2018

By Jennifer Reynolds
Copyright

1-6846746841

ISBN-13: 978-0-9778335-3-5

ISBN-10: 0-9778335-3-4

ROBIN WOOD TAROT – COPYRIGHT ROBIN WOOD © 1991

DECK USED WITH PERMISSION

Opinions and definitions expressed are those of the author only.

See Tarot Readings: Book of Combinations Vol 1 and Vol 2

Contents

Introduction..3
Inheritance from a woman..............................6
Bad background chec....................................8
Brooding girl goes to her dad........................10
Flooded car. Angry at God............................12
Metastasized uterine cancer..........................14
Making a legal settlement.............................16
Do not buy that house..................................18
Pet thinks guy hurt him.................................20
What will I be seeing in the news...................22
Wife thinks husband is cheating....................24
The girlfriend is cheating..............................26
Child born with defects.................................28
Laid off from their job...................................30
Marriage delayed for prenuptials...................32
Will they get their money back......................34
House catches fire with total loss..................36
Nephew is stealing from his aunt...................38
The baby abused by the babysitter................40
Breaking new ground in the metaphysical.....42
Tarot reading saves them from buying bad....44
Great business idea, but beware of document..............46
Protesting after police encounter...................48
Seeking wisdom and the mind of God............50
Reading for a cat..52
Past life reading...54
Unconventional writing. Retiring....................56
Will candidate #1 win the election? Answer: No.........58
Will candidate # 2 win the election? Answer: Yes..........60
Do they really love me 62
Birthdates..64
Major Arcana...66
    SWORDS...77
    CUPS..84
    WANDS...91
    PENTACLES..98
    Medical Definitions of Cards....................105
Bonus...108

BLANK PAGE

Introduction

Thank you for purchasing this book of tarot layouts. I would like to take a moment to explain how to use this book. I have put together a series of layouts, which are explained card by card according to their position and their associations to other cards. You are also reminded of other definitions for the cards but suggestions are made as to why one definition is chosen over another. Other interpretations for the card combinations are given to encourage you to think along the lines of other possibilities. In this way much more knowledge is obtained from each layout, expanding upon the training experience.

The purpose of this book is to help train your mind, to develop a certain pattern of thinking as I guide you along through my own thought processes in a consistent manner while trying to be as thorough as possible. I have tried to make the layouts interesting while keeping them realistic. The layouts are drawn from over 20 years of experience, thinking about readings I have personally done so that what I present has already been proven-out.

You probably have never done tarot readings in the manner presented in this book. You might not have realized that a tarot reading could provide such specific information that actually applies to everyday life. This system makes tarot readings more practical and applicable and therefore more helpful to the client (and for your own readings).

I have two other tarot books and have been careful not to duplicate combinations. *"Tarot Readings: Book of Combinations Vol 1"* contains all card definitions followed by 628 two and three card combinations and a fun quiz with key. It would make a great supplement to this book. Volume 2 does not repeat the card definitions but has over 800 two card combinations. I may do one more book of layouts in the future but it will be awhile.

After the series of 30 layouts in this book, I have included the definitions of the major and minor tarot cards. They are the same as in my other book, volume 1, so that you do not need to purchase that book as well, unless you are interested in studying its card combinations.

There are plenty of great layouts and I encourage you to try different ones to see what you like. The Celtic Cross is a popular one so we will use it just for consistence sake. In the sample below, I have numbered the cards to show their sequence in the layout and their positions based on past, present, future, environment and thinking. The 3 card cut is at the top and are used as added information regarding the current situation and can relate to the present, the past or the future. You can read these cards from left to right, right to left, or from center.

Inheritance from a woman.

The first card is Justice, that lets us know this is about a legal issue. It could be things like courts, attorneys, bail bondsmen, or legal documents. Cross that is the Wheel of Fortune. This looks like a legal big win, either in luck or money. In the right column is the Empress. She represents an older relative, like a mother, ones grandparents or aunts and uncles. These three cards are in the "present" position. Taking these cards together, it looks like we are seeing an inheritance from an elder family member or their mother. What cards you chose to read next depends on where your attention is drawn, there is no hard and fast rule. This allows the reading to be open to intuition.

I am drawn to the two cards in the past position, the 6 of Cups for children or childhood and the Hermit for looking at, searching for, or counseling. It appears that someone has been looking for the children of the elder who are heirs to her inheritance.

In the "Environment" position is the 6 of Swords. This shows a trip. This suggests that handling the inheritance is going to require travel.

Continuing up the right column to the "Thinking" position is the Page of Swords for urgent news. This alludes to the swiftness of thought. You will notice that her feet don't touch the ground.

In the three future positions are the King of Swords, the 9 of Wands, and the 9 of Cups. Take your time to ponder these cards. Your mind will run through several scenarios. It is okay to present several possibilities without having to commit to just one. This way you don't rule out other potential possibilities that are just as viable. This is actually better for the client because this allows them to be alert on many fronts without locking them in to only one scenario and miss something.

Readings are like putting together a puzzle where you turn a piece this way and that until it makes more sense.

The King of Swords is usually an actual male, more so than an attribute. He can be an air sign male, a surgeon, a writer. As a surgeon, he has a scalpel in his hand. As a writer he has a pen in his hand. We have to look at the other two cards to see what he is doing here.

The 9 of Wands shows someone standing their ground, ready to do battle. They plan to defend their position. The 9 of Cups shows someone being happy or having friendly intentions. Taking these three cards together, it appears to me that this male is defending the client's best interest and that he is going to stand up for them in the inheritance proceedings. He would be their ally.

In the three cards cut, upper left, are 8 of Pentacles for reading, writing, or documents, the Ace of Pentacles for large sum of money, and 8 of Wands for swiftly. This reads that there has been or will be a letter regarding a sum of money, either gained or lost, that has occurred very quickly, or that brings advances. Taking into consideration the rest of the reading, this is probably the letter of notice regarding the family inheritance.

Bad background check.

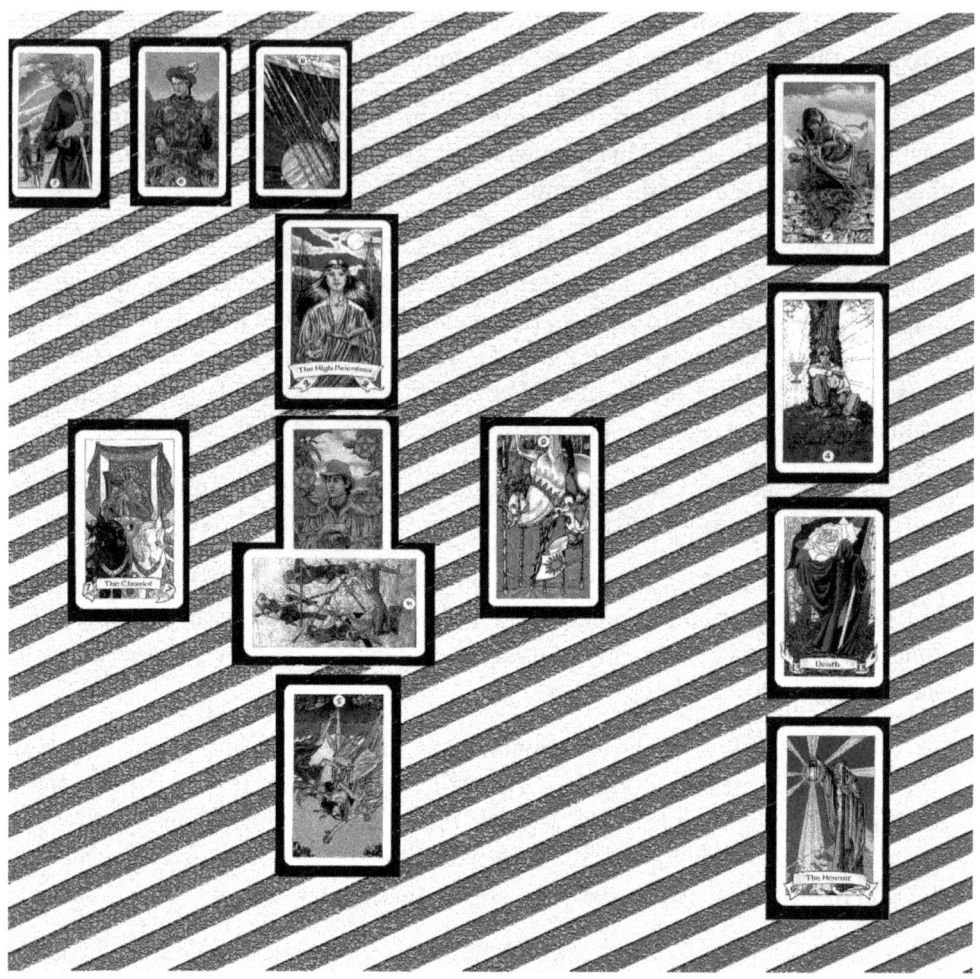

The first card is the 7 of Pentacles indicating a job, but it can also mean a time of fruition after much work. Crossing that is the 5 of Wands that generally means worry or thinking a lot about something. The first card in the right column is the Hermit showing that something is being looked at or searched for, but can also mean giving counsel or advice. Taking these three cards together, it appears that the client is worried about a job that they are searching for, or worried about something coming to light about their job. Like all combinations, it can be read different ways.

The next card in the column, in the Environment position, is the Death card. Something is being blocked or comes to an end. It appears that the job situation they are worried about is being blocked or ended. The next card, in the Thinking position is the 4 of Cups. The client, or person the reading is for, is not satisfied or may be sulking. It indicates how they are feeling about the subject being considered.

In the three future positions are the High Priestess, the reversed 6 of Wands and the 7 of Swords. We will consider the possibilities of each card separately, then try to piece them together. The High Priestess refers to things of a confidential nature, secrets, hidden knowledge, a diary, personal accounts, classified files, or intuition and psychic activity. The reversed 6 of Wands indicates something or someone not being well received, having a bad reputation or character. Someone or "something" is not being honored. The 7 of Swords is all manner of criminal activity or evil intent.

You see that, as can be expected, the definitions for these three cards have cast a somewhat broad net. In order to narrow the meaning down, you must go back to the situation that was indicated by the first three cards. It is very rare that the three "Future" positions are not related. Sometimes they aren't related to the situation at hand, but most of the time they are.

I relayed to the client that the cards indicate a job that is either being searched for or that is being looked in to. She told me that she had applied for a job and they were doing a background check. She was worried about what they would find. We were on the right track. I immediately see the High Priestess as the record containing her personal criminal history. The reversed 6 of Wands shows that her reputation and character has been tarnished and the 7 of Swords shows that this background check will contain criminal history.

Looking at the two cards in the past position, we see Chariot for vehicle and reversed 3 of Cups, the classic combination for drinking and driving. I simply asked, *"Were you drinking and driving"*. She admitted that she had a DUI and she went on to tell what happened. I explained how the cards showed that this was going to come up in her background check. She then understood why they were not calling her back. Nothing is going to come from this job application and is why the Death card is in the Environment position.

On the three card cut we have the 5 of Swords for troubles and difficulties, but can also mean someone stabbing you in the back or taking unfair advantage. And, the 6 of Pentacles for giving and receiving, but also indicates dispersing payments and paying the bills. And the reversed 8 of Wands is lack of advancement or progress, or things related to speed (either too slow or too fast). Upright, it can mean to transverse (travel) a long distance. Again, these cards usually are keeping in line with the subject of the layout, but sometimes are on a different subject.

I read it as her having difficulty but still paying the bills but that there is no immediate prospect of things getting any better for quite some time.

Brooding girl goes to her dad.

    The first card is the 4 of Cups for disappointed, sulking, or brooding. Cross that is the reversed Fool (facing right). The definitions for the Fool run along the lines of a simple person, a slow learner, having a mental disability, or just feeling stupid. Or, indicates a person is innocent or unaware. It can represent being naive or gullible. It also means something that is new, either a new object or a new venture. It also indicates being inexperienced. In the right column is the reversed 6 of Pentacles and refers to reading, writing, documents, courses, training, and school. Knowing that the reading is for a child, I can assume reversed relates to problems in school or homework. The client confirmed that her daughter is moody, has trouble learning, and does not like school. She was not doing her work and was making poor grades.

    In the environment is the Lovers card. My attention is drawn to the King of Swords. There is definitely a male in the equation. He can be an air sign male, a solider (gun in hand), surgeon (scalpel in hand), or writer (pen in hand). Also, in the past is the World card. The World generally means completion, all encompassing, a thing in its entirety, but can also be interstate travel and flying. At the time, many young boys in the area had joined the military to fight in the Iraq war. Taking into consideration the reading was for a teenage girl, it was safe to assume this was a soldier who had either just left or recently returned home.

I tell the mom, *"The past is saying a soldier that flew."* She was surprised and shared that a boy had just flown back from Iraq just to see her daughter. I then said, *"Oh, that's why the Lovers card is here,"* and I left it at that. The Lovers card shows they are in a relationship but it is important to know that it does not <u>prove</u> they are having sex! The closest you can come to proving someone is having sex is if you turn the Lovers card upside down and still pull it into the layout

In the Thinking position is the 7 of Cups. It represents unrealistic thinking, fantasy, imagining, or a misunderstanding. But it can also refer to artistic things like paintings and photographs because these things require imagination.

The girl had become obsessed with the idea of her father who had been out of their lives for years. She expressed romanticized ideas about how wonderful her father was and had become obsessed at looking through old photographs of him, staring at them for long hours. She even placed the photographs around the house. This is an instance of a card doing "double duty". Two of its definitions were being expressed; the girl's unrealistic fantasy about her father, and the pictures she had become obsessed with.

The three future cards are the 9 of Wands, the 6 of Swords, and the King of Cups. We can now safely take into consideration what we know about the situation so far, yet tentatively keeping an open mind. It's risky to lock the cards in to one outcome. What I like to say is that the cards are never wrong. The problem lies in how they are interpreted.

The 9 of Wands shows the girl being stubborn and not backing down. She is ready to do battle. The 6 of Swords shows her traveling or leaving. And the King of Cups represents her father. The King of Cups also means a water-sign male or a doctor, but we know that it is her father. The likely scenario is that after a confrontation, she is going to leave to go be with her father, who in her mind she has idolized.

On the cut are the Page of Cups, reversed Page of Swords, and two of Swords. The Page of Cups is usually a young girl, or any creative child full of wonder, or adult who is sweet and childlike. The reversed Page of Swords is an unruly or hyperactive child (or adult). And the 2 of Swords is a crossroads or decision. I read this as the daughter acting out and things finally coming to a head where a decision is made, which is her leaving for her father.

Flooded car. Angry at God.

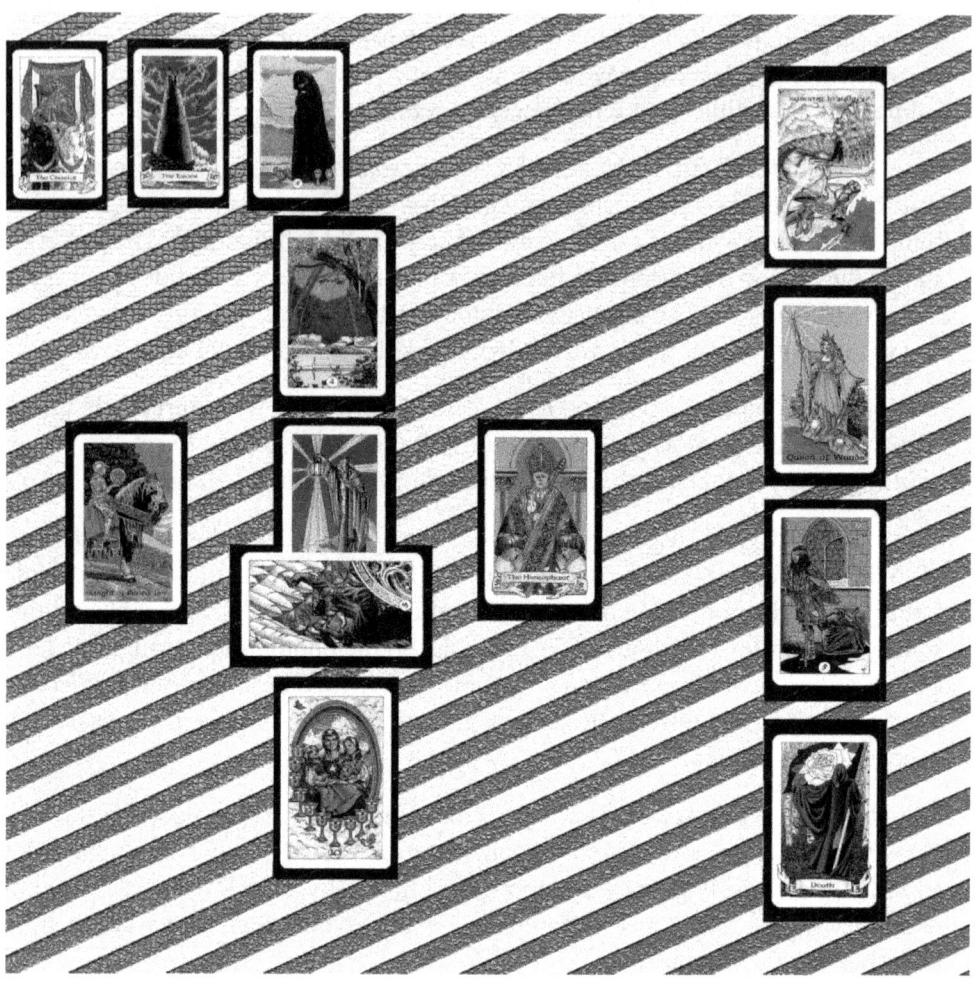

    This was a general reading and not on anything specific. It was for my brother, which gives me an advantage. When you first start reading, it is good to practice on friends and family. Most will *love* for you to read for them.

    The first card is Hermit, and crossing is 3 of Pentacles, which is usually a job, but can mean "working on something". The Hermit can mean consulting, advising, seeking, guiding, and can mean aged or old. My brother does contract work, which makes him a consultant (as a computer programmer). He is also an older gray haired guy who works with a lot of younger people. This made him feel like he doesn't fit in. He had thought about looking for another job. So, you see that all of these definitions can fit this combination: job as a consultant, being the older guy at work, and seeking a new job.

In the right column is the Death card. This position relates to the first two cards. It helps narrow down their meaning. I said, *"Whatever is going on with your job, you can forget it. It isn't going anywhere, it's a dead end."* And I pointed to the Death card. He replied that it confirmed what he had been suspecting, that his job was going to play out. I advised him to save his money in case it did.

In the environment position is the 5 of Pentacles and shows he is having health issues. The card can also mean abuse and rejection but I know these don't apply to him. He has had heart by-pass surgery, is diabetic with high blood pressure, all of which he doesn't take proper care of.

In the thinking position is the Queen of Wands. This could be his on-again, off-again girlfriend, who is red haired. In another layout he was trying to figure out how to fix their relationship. It is not related to his job but she is what he has been thinking of more than his job situation.

In the past are 10 of Cups for happy family relations and Knight of Pentacles which can be either money or just offering help in some way. This reads that their family as recently given them a loan or has helped them out.

The Future cards are 4 of Swords (bed), Hierophant (religion), and reversed Knight of Swords (angry). Some form of this combination was showing up in all his readings and I already knew what it meant. My brother is angry at God and blames Him for the crime, suffering, and corruption on this planet and he complains about this at night while lying in bed. I have counseled him many times for long hours. I explain that God is not an external entity but is in all of creation, including within us and how this negative energy could be affecting his health and destroying his cardiovascular system. He admits that it is wrong and promises to stop.

On the cut is the Chariot, Tower, and 5 of Cups. It is a classic combination for having car problems, although there are other ways to interpret the Chariot, one being a control issue. You could even read this as, "having lost control of their vehicle". But, what had happened was that he got caught in a flood that hit Houston and drove into high water. The Tower card is the bad weather card for things like floods, fires, earthquakes, storms, tornados, and the like. The car was ruined and the motor had to be replaced. The cost was close to 6 thousand dollars, of which I, a family member, loaned him (past position).

So, you see how it all fits, even though I had the home-team advantage. You also notice that there are three things going on in this layout. One, his job situation, two, his anger at God while lying in bed, and three, his car disaster.

Metastasized cancer.

      This is a health reading. You will need to switch gears. Even if you didn't intend to do a health reading, a clue that it is a health reading is the reversed Knight of Swords (facing right).The reversed Knight of Swords can mean angry or cancer. Research has shown that the energy of habitual anger can lead to cancer. The Empress is usually their mother, a wife, or "mother of their children", or an elder relative. If you aren't thinking "health reading" your first instinct is to read this as being angry at their mother (wife, or elder) or that their mother is angry about something. Even if I did not intend to do a health reading, a quick glance around the layout puts me on this trail. Specifically, in the past I see the 5 of Pentacles for health (or abuse, neglect) and the Queen of Swords for nurse, a healer, or places you go for healings, such as clinics and hospitals. Switching to a health reading changes the definition of the Empress, which in a health reading relates to abdominal problems, such as the stomach, pancreas, gallbladder, appendix, uterus, or ovaries.

In the right column is the 9 of Swords for physical or emotional pain and it can even mean both. They could be having pain related to their cancer, and they could be crying. In the environment is the 6 of Cups for children (or childhood). They don't have to be young children, they can be grown children who are coming close to support her.

In the Thinking position is 5 of Wands for worry (or giving lots of thought to a thing). This can be expected and lends to this being a health reading. You see how assigning positions in the layout, such as Environment and Thinking, helps with the reading. Just remember that what is in the Thinking position doesn't have to be an actual fact, it is just something they are thinking.

In the future positions are World, 10 of Swords, and reversed Judgement. Taking the health definition for these cards causes the World card to indicate that the cancer has metastasized, meaning it traveled through the blood stream and seeded to other organs in the body.

The 10 of Swords means devastated, but in a health reading can also mean bleeding out. Either of these or both of these could apply here. They could be bleeding from the cancer and maybe it won't stop or they are devastated about their diagnosis. The reversed Judgement means that they will not recover their health. If the Judgement card was upright, then all would be well and they would recover.

On the cut is Page of Swords for urgent news, 5 of Cups for grief and loss, and reversed 4 of Swords for being bedbound, maybe even a hospice bed.

This health reading is being provided for those who are interested. But remember, you cannot diagnose or offer medical advice. You can say things like, it looks like or might be and advise them to always refer to a doctor. I saved my mother's best friends life just by telling her that it looked like she had a circulation problem in her neck (reversed World and Hanged Man). I told her that if she felt anything at all in her neck to not ignore it but go to the doctor immediately. Within days she felt something in her neck move and went to the ER and had emergency surgery. If she had gone to bed, she would have died. So, there are ways to do a health reading without diagnosing or prescribing treatment.

Making a legal settlement.

    Start with a quick glance around the layout. This keeps you from having to go back when you come across one card that changes everything. The card that jumps out to me is the Justice card. This tells me that there has been a legal issue going on. And, the Hanged Man tells me that it has been in limbo. So, you see that you don't have to start the reading with the first two cards. I would clarify my suspicions by asking them, *"Have you been involved with a legal issue?"*

    If they say yes, then I continue the reading in that vein. This helps narrow the rest of the reading. The 2 of Pentacles means deliberating on a thing, the actual balance of a thing, a balancing act such as trying to handle multiple things at once, the exchange of two things such as one thing for another, or an electronic transfer of money across the wires. I quickly run through these definitions while keeping in mind the legal issue. How could this card relate to a legal issue?

Now that I have called up the definition of the 2 of Pentacles into the forefront of my mind, I move on to the 2 of Cups and the Knight of Cups. The 2 of Cups shows an amicable agreement and means things like friendship, partnering, and merger, or even the mixing of things together. It has been shown to represent a cell phone because two people can connect on it. Feel free to come up with new meanings for a card.

The Knight of Cups means an opportunity or offer. It also means a romantic relationship. Keeping in mind the legal issue that has been in limbo, I take these three cards to mean that after a deliberation (2 of Pents), all things being considered, that an agreement is made (2 of Cups) and an offer is presented (Knight of Cups).

In the environment is Ace of Pentacles. There is definitely money. In the Thinking position is the 5 of Swords. Remember, this may or may not be real. This card means trouble and difficulties, others taking advantage, sabotage, a bully and paranoia. It reflects how they have been feeling about the situation.

In the Future positions are Ace of Swords. It puts a very positive spin on anything and also means the answer is yes. The 8 of Cups shows them being able to leave this situation behind and the 7 of Wands shows success.

The cut has 8 of Swords for feeling trapped or restricted, the 7 of Cups for imaginings, and the Strength card. Strength usually means just that, but in this case considering the other two cards, I am going to take its reversed definition, which is okay to do, and say that it is fear. They have been feeling stuck (8 of Swords) and probably imagining the worst (7 of Cups), so there is likely an element of fear (rev. Strength). But, everything will turn out fine in the final outcome card (7 of Wands).

The Strength card has been a hard card for me to grasp in general. I finally decided that it means a person is very kind, caring, gentle, and considerate. They are accepting and non-judgmental, a humanitarian type person who would be careful to make you feel comfortable and welcome.

Do not buy that house.

Buying a house isn't something you can easily back out of once the purchase is made. A lot of stress is involved. This is a time when you wish you had a crystal ball to look into, well tarot can be just that. I have had the opportunity to do multiple readings on home purchases in my twenty years as a reader. And although I do not get it all into this layout, one home was a total nightmare. It had electrical problems (Sun card). Instead of a breaker box, it had a fuse box! The well was dry (Emperor for drought) and it cost $15,000 to dig a new one. The stove and water heater went out (Rev Ace Pentacles for mechanical problems). The roof leaked (4 of Wands for structure problems). It was haunted (Hanged Man) by the previous owner, a grouchy old man who died in the house and didn't want anyone there. And worst of all, the neighbor was a raging alcoholic who spewed curses at them while waving a gun and threatened their very lives (King of Swords). Poor thing went into foreclosure the first year *and* ruined her credit! Unfortunately, she had come to me after the fact. A reading could have saved her from misery because the main benefit of a tarot reading is to <u>prevent</u> things from happening. You can change the outcome. The layout example I give is a little different than the situation just described.

The 10 of Pentacles for house or building (also apartments, office, and even a single room) is crossed by the 9 of Pentacles representing the grounds, the yard, or the area. It is reversed (facing right) to show there is a problem with securing the area, and the 9 of Swords shows there is criminal activity involved. In the Environment position is the 6 of Swords. Knowing what I know about the criminal activity, it makes me think that someone is returning to the house, possibly having lived there before or knew someone who lived there before.

Looking to the future positions, I see the Devil card, which can mean drugs (prescription or street drugs) or a toxic situation, and the reversed King of Swords for a neurotic and dangerous male. The 5 of Swords shows that they are going to have problems out of him. The advice would be to check with the police department regarding calls to make sure this wasn't a previous drug house or if there were problems with the neighbor. They should also drive by late at night and on the weekends to see what is happening.

In the Thinking position is the Star card. It indicates that owning a home has been their dream, their hope, and their ultimate goal. Reversed would show it crushed. In the past are the Page of Wands and the 4 of Pentacles. The Page of Wands represents buying and selling because it is something you make an announcement about and advertise, usually using computers and other types of media. And the 4 of Pentacles means taking possession of, wanting to keep or hang on to something. You might know it as meaning greed, but it is much broader than that. It can mean keeping something locked way from prying eyes, like a safe or safety deposit box, or keeping a person safe. It looks to me that they were set on buying this particular house and were saying, *"I really want it!"*

On the cut is the King of Pentacles for banks and loans (also savings accounts, credit unions, 401ks, stocks, bonds, and CDs). 9 of Cups shows them happy, and 2 of Wands shows them looking forward to their goals in life. 2 of Wands also means having good self-esteem. This cut shows that they are happy that they got the bank loan they needed to realize their goals.

But, what is alarming about this layout is the 7 of Swords, the reversed King of Swords, the Devil card and the 5 of Swords. The more negative cards, the worse it is, and there is a preponderance of bad cards in this layout; enough that I would feel comfortable advising against buying this particular house, no matter how cute or "perfect" they think it is.

Pet thinks guy hurt him.

Pet readings are interesting and a nice treat for pet owners. The first thing I notice, which is easy, is the Ace of Cups and Queen of Cups. The pet really loves this woman. She is kind and nurturing. With the easy part out of the way, I take on the more difficult challenges of the Moon card, the reversed Ace of Swords and the King of Swords. The sure thing in this combination is that there is a male figure. He can be an air-sign. Taking the reversed meaning, he can be a neurotic male. Or, he can be a Vet because he can represent a surgeon. Or, he can be a soldier.

Next, I ponder the Moon card. This card is complex. It is all kinds of mental illness (dementia, memory loss, bipolar, PTSD, schizophrenia, strokes, seizures, etc.'). Or, things are not as they seem and might be an illusion. It can refer to our shadow side, meaning things that drive us that are hidden from our conscious. Also, Moon means any growth (tumors, warts, moles, boils, pimples).

The Ace of swords reversed can mean a hostile situation, even war, negative and critical thinking, or sharp pain. These three cards can read: tumor, sharp pain, vet. Or: mental illness, hostile situation, neurotic male. Or: PTSD, war, Soldier. Or: illusion, pain, air-sign male. Take a moment to consider these various definitions.

Ask some clarifying questions from the client. You could say, *"I see a male, he could be an air-sign, a soldier, or maybe a Vet. Does your pet have tumors?"* In this case, she had a spouse who was an air sign and who loved their cat. I said, *"It looks like the pet thinks that he hurt it"*.

The cat was 20 years old and in renal failure, his bones hurt. He had tried to jump up on the bed when the husband grabbed him to help. The cat felt a sharp pain and thought that he had caused it. The cat yelled and took to avoiding him for a while. The news of the reading broke their hearts and she promised that they would both love up extra on the cat.

In the Environment position is the 7 of Cups. This is misunderstandings, imagination, fantasy, false perceptions, hallucinations, or can be artistic endeavors. But, it is also smoke and odors, a heavy cigarette smoker. Since this is a pet, I am going to guess that there is something in the environment that is disturbing their sensitive sense of smell. I asked if they smoked, used strong cleansers, or sprays. Neither smoked but she used carpet freshner. She would stop.

In the Thinking position is the 10 of Wands. That can mean a heavy load, working hard, carrying a burden, or responsibilities. But as a medical card, this means difficulty walking. Of course being an old cat, I understood that the cat was wondering why it hurts to walk. I suggested a heating pad for the cat and was told later that he really loved it.

In the three future positions are the reversed 4 of Swords, the 4 of Cups, and the Page of Wands. Reversed 4 of Swords is difficulty sleeping, no bed, sleeping too much, or being bed bound. The 4 of Cups is not being happy with something, sulking or brooding. And the Page of Wands is buying or selling, making announcements, advertisements, computers, radio, television, and noise, etc'. It goes without saying that many of these won't apply to a pet, which actually makes the reading easier. I know that cats sleep a lot, mostly during the day. So, it appears that his sleep is being disturbed by noise. It could be people talking, dogs barking, loud music or television, or a disruptive home.

Another interpretation is that the cat is meowing plaintively, trying to complain about their bed. The elderly cat had become weak and it was difficult for him to jump, so they bought him a cat bed for the floor and he was happy.

On the cut is 10 of Pentacles, 9 of Cups and 3 of Cups. This simply shows that they are happy with their home and their food.

What will I be seeing in the news?

Reading the news is another specialized area, like medical or pet readings. You have to shift your thinking. News readings are not going to be as specific in details. You won't get names or locations but you can be pretty sure it's going to be something bad. You can however, pin down a time frame by narrowing repeated readings and move up and down to a specific week or day and see how things change. Many times I have gotten an event down to the very date.

The first card is the Page of Swords to represent news, which is usually of a sudden or urgent nature. Crossing that is the 10 of Swords, meaning devastation. In the right column is the 7 of Cups. This reads, urgent news related to devastation caused by things like smoke, fog, toxic fumes, and air pollutants. There could be ash fallout from a volcano, an ammonia plant might blow up, the pollen count could be bad, people might be trapped by smoke, forest fires could affect visibility. At this point, the list goes on and on. In the Environment is the Knight of Swords. Since this is a disaster, the obvious meaning is rescue personnel; police, ambulances, rangers, military, helicopters, divers, rescue boats.

In the past are Tower and Death card. I have said that the Death card rarely means actual death unless there are other negative cards present. Well, this is one of those cases. In the Thinking position is the reversed Star card. This means hopes and dreams dashed. But, it also means anything that falls down from the sky, things like meteors, airplanes, hail, ash, even the space shuttle. Remember how I said that since this is the Thinking position that it isn't necessarily real? Well, scratch that. We aren't reading on a person, we are reading the news. Something falls from the sky.

In the future positions are 5 of Cups for grief and loss, and the 8 of Cups for evacuations. People have to leave everything behind. The 4 of Pentacles in this case would be a safe haven, a place where they have hunkered down, like storm shelters, bomb shelters, auditoriums, and FEMA camps or tent cities.

In the cut is the 8 of Swords for trapped, Ace of Wands for fire or explosion, and 3 of Swords for killed. The 3 of Swords is the most catastrophic card in the deck, bar none. The Ace of Wands is the only card in this layout that indicates what we might be dealing with and this is a fire or explosion, both of which would cause significant smoke. It could be a massive building fire where people are trapped on floors. It could be a bombing, which would be an explosion and a fire. A chemical plant could explode. This would contaminate the air and cause evacuations.

See what I mean about reading the news being much more difficult, especially with today's global news and there being disasters happening around the world on a daily basis. If I wanted to pursue this, I would double down on my focus and intent, like zeroing in, fine tuning. And I would do multiple layouts and I would take pictures of the layouts. I would begin to parse and analyze the layouts, looking for clues, hoping to get a card that leaves no doubt. Maybe the Chariot, telling me there is a vehicle involved, including 18 wheelers, trains, subways, boats and planes. Or the 10 of Pentacles, telling me there are buildings involved. The reversed Knight of Swords would tell me it is a terroristic act. The reversed Page of Wands would tell me that there was no advanced warning, or communications are lost. The 5 of Swords or 7 of Swords would mean it is a deliberate act. The Queen of Pentacles represents mother earth so could be a natural disaster. The Devil card would indicate the smoke is toxic or poison, like nerve gas or ammonia. You get the idea.

Every card counts. You might get a significant piece of information only once! If you want to get good at reading the news, you need to practice and keep a record. Going back over readings is very helpful in learning how the cards communicate information. It is how they have taught me.

Wife thinks husband is cheating.

Cheating is part of the human dynamics, probably from the beginning of time. It's a touchy subject and up to you if you want to do these types of readings or tell the client when you see it, because, you know… what if you're wrong? The cards are never wrong but you could read it wrong. These kinds of readings call for some finesse, some delicacy. The first card is the 4 of Wands indicating a marriage. It can also mean a wedding is taking place. Next is the 9 of Wands showing a defensive action. To the right is the Devil card indicating a toxic situation is happening in the marriage. It could be that by trying to defend her marriage she is the one causing their relationship to become toxic. For example, her saying things like, *"Where were you? Who were you talking to? You don't love me anymore! You're cheating on me, I just know it!"*

This could also read that they have a defensive attitude that they have to win some battle and won't back down and this is what is harming their marriage.

The past shows a happy family life and children. So, there is nothing there to set precedence or triggering source, like an old girlfriend or unhappy family life. In the Environment is the 2 of Swords, so obviously someone is about to make a major decision or change in course. Could she be planning to take action on her suspicions of him cheating? In the Thinking position is the reversed Lovers card, the classic card for cheating. But again, remember it is in the Thinking position and therefore cannot be taken as real (unless you are reading the news).

In the future positions are the King of Cups, Fool, and 10 of Wands. The King of Cups is probably her husband (not water-sign male, father, or doctor). And the Fool card means that he is not doing anything nefarious. He is innocent of her suspicions. In fact, he is seen working hard in the 10 of Wands. He is carrying his responsibilities and keeping his nose to the grindstone, so to speak. The long shadow of the setting sun precedes him as he heads home after a long day's work. Shame on his wife for thinking he has been cheating.

In the cut are the Moon card, the Queen of Cups, and the 7 of Cups. The Queen of Cups would be her, the wife, and both the Moon and the 7 of Cups indicate her imagination is running wild. The Moon and 7 of Cups both showing up together just compounds the message of delusions that are not real. But, a word of caution here is that the Moon card also represents all types of mental illnesses, including early onset dementia. Dementia causes people to become paranoid and suspicious. They are delusional and hallucinate. It is very frightful for them. It isn't just a disease of forgetfulness. Dementia patients are difficult to deal with and can become violent. They don't trust even their closest relatives. So, remember this if you see this combination.

There isn't enough in the reading to say that the wife is suffering from early onset dementia and as with all health readings, you cannot diagnose without a medical license because you are not a doctor (unless you really are a doctor). I've mentioned elsewhere that I am a retired critical care nurse and even I cannot diagnose. Only doctors can diagnose. I cannot prescribe treatment either. I can only suggest a possibility and advise them to seek a medical doctor's opinion. One way to approach the possibility of early onset dementia with the wife would be to tell it as a story, even if not true. *"You know, I had an aunt who thought my uncle was cheating and he wasn't. She was later diagnosed with early onset dementia."* And very quickly move on. It's up to you and how comfortable you are with the client.

The girlfriend is cheating

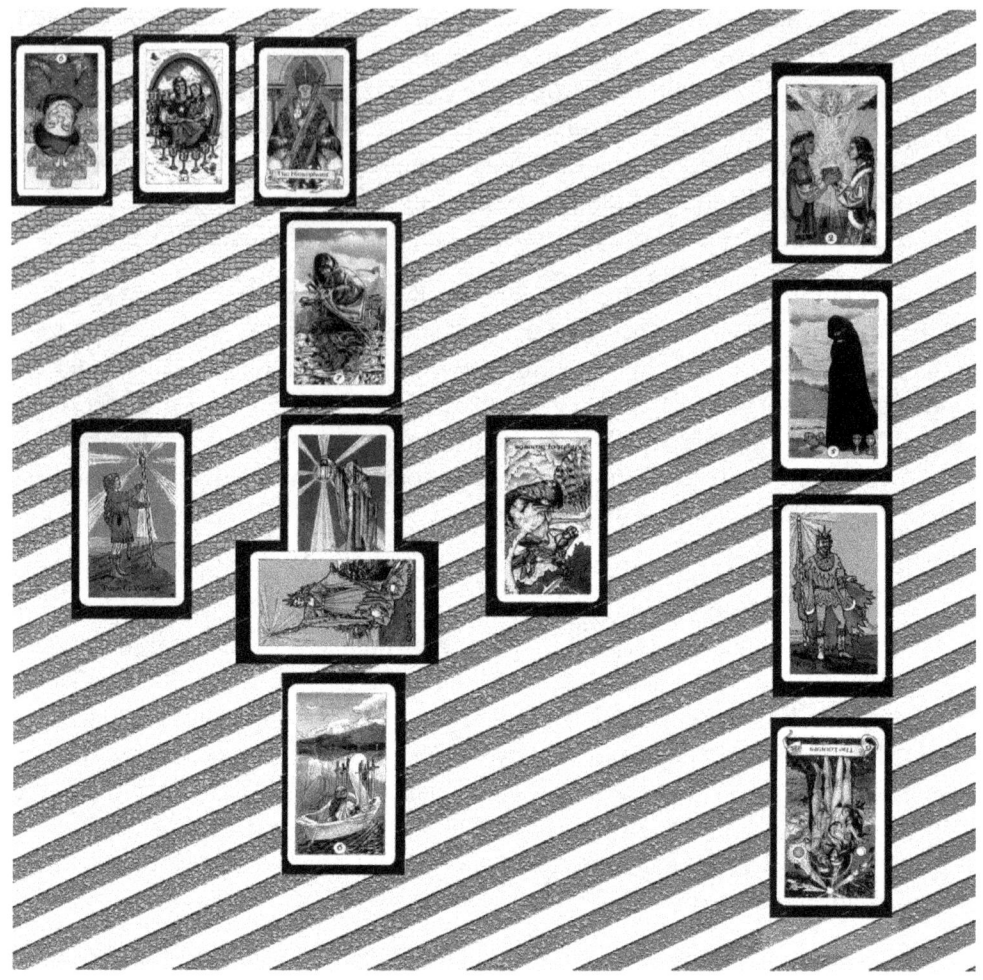

    The previous layout on cheating showed that the husband wasn't cheating, so what would it look like if someone was cheating? There are classic cards you would get. But remember, not getting the expected cards are just as important in a reading. Not getting a card that indicates cheating usually means they aren't cheating. The cards are drawn by the laws of attraction. The energy around cheating would draw the card to them. And if the card shows up again and again then you can take it to the bank.

    The first card is the Hermit and the second card is the Queen of Wands. Someone is looking into this woman (or searching for her). To the right is the reversed Lovers card. She is cheating. That means the Hermit could be saying that her cheating has come to light, been discovered or exposed. The Hermit could also be a private investigator or surveillance cameras. Wouldn't that be interesting?

In the Environment is the King of Wands. This is probably her lover, especially if her current boyfriend is not a "fire-sign male". The King of Wands can also represent an ex-boyfriend. The question then becomes, is she seeing an old boyfriend or a fire-sign male?

In the Thinking position is the 5 of Cups for grief and loss, as expected. If the 3 of Swords were here, it would indicate heartbreak. Heartbreak is much worse than grief and loss. 3 of Swords is also "kill". Be careful that the 3 of Swords doesn't indicate, *"I'm going to kill her"*. Keep in mind that a cheating partner can make a person crazy and do things they would never do otherwise. That is why you have to be very careful. You also wouldn't want to cause a divorce with the client going home and telling their partner that their tarot reader just said they were cheating! Be aware of the ramifications of your readings.

In the past are the Page of Wands and the 6 of Swords. This looks like someone giving them a call to come and meet them. This includes instant messaging, texts, Instagram, and even Facebooking. The trip is being made specifically for their encounter.

In the Future positions are the 7 of Swords, the reversed Knight of Swords, and the final outcome is the 2 of Cups. The 7 of Swords is a card specific for cheating. Betrayal is a criminal act and a violation of trust. The reversed Knight of Swords means anger. So, our client is angry about the betrayal. But look what happens. They make up. The 2 of Cups show they remain friends. They have forgiven her. It isn't our place to judge. It would not be professional to tell them to leave them or what they should and shouldn't do. That is not our place as a reader. A trained therapist would never tell their patients what to do, much less a tarot reader. We should support the client in whatever they decide. This means we maintain a standard of ethics that also includes confidentiality. You do not share readings with their friends and family or co-workers.

On the cut is the reversed 9 of Cups, the 10 of Cups and the Hierophant. It points to another problem with the relationship and that is that one or the other's family (10 Cups) is not happy or not being friendly towards them (rev. 9 Cups) because the partner is not of the same race, religion, or culture (Hierophant). Or, this is a gay relationship. The Hierophant indicates things that goes against tradition, its reversed meaning, and it is a card that many times takes on its reversed meaning even if it shows up in the readings as upright.

Child born with birth defects.

     Three baby cards are in this layout, the Empress, the Ace of Wands and the Sun card. In all three instances, there appears to be a problem. In the Past positions the reversed Empress is with the 4 of Swords. There appears to be a problem with the pregnant mother and the 4 of Swords suggests she is put on bedrest. Of course, other ways to interpret this combination could be an elder who is sleeping too much or who is bedridden. If the 4 of Swords was reversed the elder could have insomnia and be up all night, not have a place to sleep, or they could even have bedbugs.

     Moving around the layout we have another baby card, the Sun, in the three card cut with the reversed Wheel of Fortune, and the 9 of Swords. The Sun card, even though not reversed, is flanked by two cards that indicate a problem with the baby. This reads that there has been an unfortunate turn of events with the baby that has brought tears.

The first card is the reversed Ace of Wands. Upright is creative forces and is usually positive and full of explosive energy. But, the Ace of Wands covers a multitude of health problems. Thankfully, we are able to narrow it down in this layout because we are dealing with a pregnancy and birth. Actually, the Ace of Wands is the birth card. But because it is reversed, it indicates a birth defect, usually genetic. Robin Wood added the DNA spiral inside the wand and the card is a phallic symbol. This will help you remember its definition.

The second card is the Fool reversed (facing right) and one of its medical definitions is mental retardation and learning disabilities. To the right is the 5 of Pentacles and supports the interpretation of being health problems with the baby.

In the Environment is the upright Judgement card. In a health reading it indicates recovery, or that they will live. In the Thinking position is the reversed 6 of Wands. 6 of Wands is about a person's reputation and how well they are being received. It is also about being triumphant. Being reversed, it suggests that the birth of a handicapped child will be hard for them to take. They are afraid of how the baby will be accepted either by the family, their spouse, or even society. Maybe the birth reflects negatively on them as a person. They don't want this reputation.

In the Future positions are the King of Cups, probably the baby's father, the reversed 4 of Pentacles and the 10 of Wands. The reversed 4 of Pentacles shows that the father doesn't want to keep the baby. He is not embracing it. But, the medical definition for the 4 of Pentacles is also problems with the arms, wrists, or hands. The 10 of Wands could be read two ways. Either he will decide to take on the responsibility despite not wanting the baby, or it is the responsibility that he doesn't want to accept. I lean more towards the 10 of Wands meaning that even though the father doesn't want the child, he will take on the responsibility, basically because the 10 of Wands card is upright.

Laid off from their job.

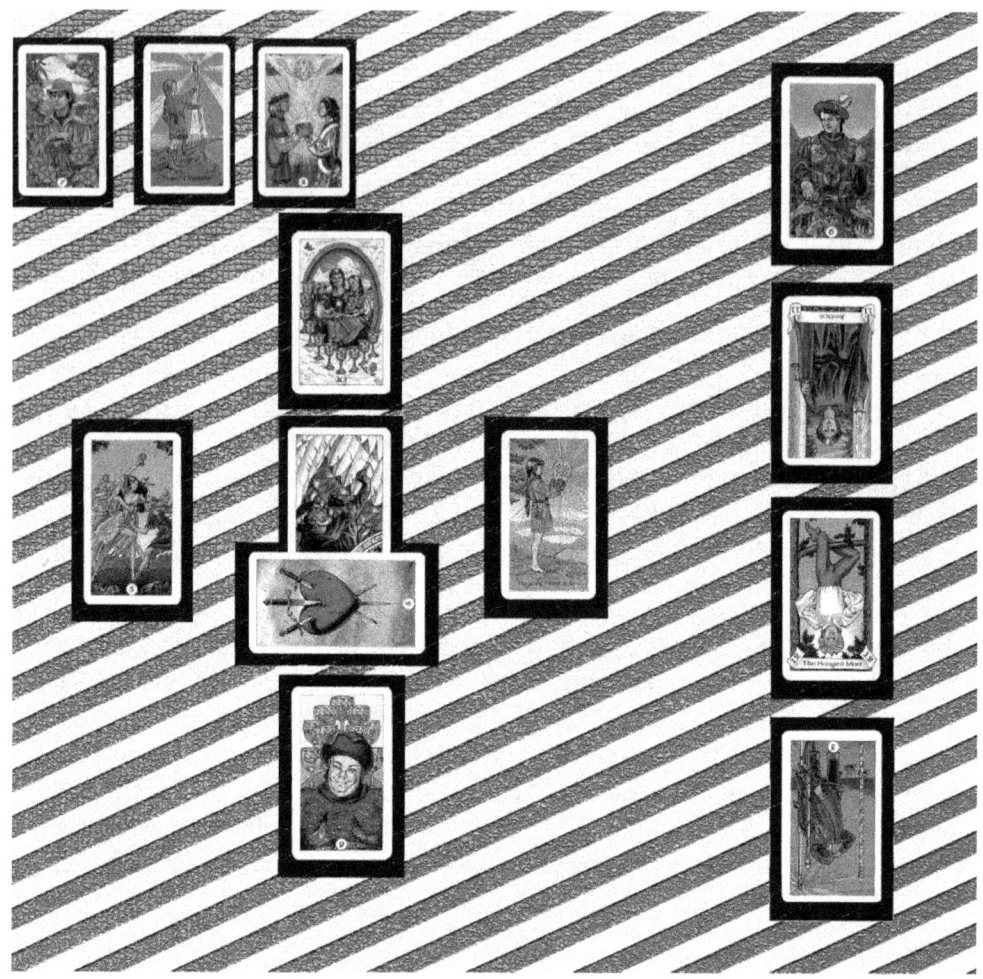

The first card is the 3 of Pentacles and usually represents a person's job but can show something being worked on. It can mean working on a file, a project, an object of durability, or anything really. Getting the card upright, you could say, *"They're working on it"*, and getting it reversed you could say, *"They aren't working on it"*. The next card is the 3 of Swords. If this were just a two card combination reading it would read, quit their job, fired from their job, laid off from their job. It could even say "being killed on their job" or that "their job is to kill". To the right is the reversed 3 of Wands and means that a business is having trouble or is going out of business. Therefore, this looks like a layoff. The upright 3 of Wands could be read as looking to network with others. It is a richly dressed merchant looking out to sea for international importing and exporting opportunities.

In the Environment position is the Hanged Man. Things are being delayed, nothing is happening and there is a sense of waiting to see, maybe waiting to hear if the layoffs will happen. In the Thinking position is the reversed Justice and indicates they feel this is unfair, or thinks that they are being discriminated against.

In the Past positions are the 3 of Cups and the 9 of Cups. Usually these two cards are something in the recent past. This combination says that just before the threat of layoff, the person was very happy and celebrating life. He might have been very happy with his job and those he worked with. The morale there would have been good. They could have just had a company picnic or party.

In the first Future position is 10 of Cups for family. They don't have to be related family, just those he is immersed with as family. A person's job may be the only family they have.

Next is the Page of Pentacles. This card is fees, payments, installments, lay-away, tuitions and dues, anything that is paid for in portions. Notice the child is holding a coin with 8 rays and this will remind you of the divisions of a whole. This card is also payments being made to, or for, a child. It can be an allowance, school tuition, student loans, school supplies, band camp, swim lessons, church camp, and school trips.

The last card is the 6 of Pentacles. It shows someone well-dressed who is handing out money to several people. This suggests that they have plenty for themselves with enough to share with others. The cards definition is "giving or receiving". It could be either. They could be receiving money or handing it out, but notice the scales, they are there to make sure they don't give away more than they can afford to or that those given to are worthy and deserving.

These future cards show that their family (10 Cups) is going to help them pay their bills (6 Pents). It's not going to be a lot, just enough to portion one bill at a time, like the electric bill here, gas money there. Or, they might pay for a child's tuition or anything related to a child's financial needs (Page Pents).

The three card cut has 7 of Pentacles, Page of Wands, and 2 of Cups. The 7 of Pentacles also represents a job and if both are in the layout it can suggest they have two jobs. This card also means a time of fruition, a time to reap the rewards of their hard work. The Page of Wands is all forms of communication and multimedia and anything that make a noise. With the 2 of Cups it shows that they are making it known to their friends that they are looking for a job (7 Pents). But, the Page of Wands plus 7 of Pents could also be them putting their Resume' out on the internet at job search sites like Indeed, Monster, and Career Builder. Then adding the 2 of Cups could mean that they have received an offer. Take a moment to consider these definitions.

Marriage delayed for prenuptials.

      The 4 of Wands is crossed by the Death card and in the right column is the Ace of Pentacles. The 4 of Wands can represent marriage. Its other definitions are a physical foundation, the foundation of a relationship or any enterprise. It can mean a venture is on solid ground or that people are in agreement towards a goal. The Death card being on the 4 of Wands shows that this marriage (or venture) will come to an end. I know that it is a marriage and not a venture by talking with the client. The Ace of Pentacles is almost always a significant amount of money. We see that the Death card functions as blocking the marriage from a sum of money.

      I see a similar card to the Death card in the Environment, which is the Hanged Man, which means things are in limbo or being delayed.

      In the Past are the Ace of Cups and Temperance. Ace of Cups means true love (a passion, or a baby) and the Temperance relates to flow, running smoothly, things being balanced, or something being easy. Temperance means equanimity, equality, level-headedness. It suggests that their love for one another is true and that it has developed without any snags, glitches, or problems. Theirs is a pretty solid relationship.

In the Thinking position is the 2 of Wands, meaning they are looking ahead towards goals in life and don't seem to be disturbed by their marriage being blocked and on hold. They are confident and self-assured.

I looked at the cards in the Future position to see if it offered me any information as to why the marriage was blocked. I opted to skip it for now and go to the three card cut. These cards are the Justice, the 8 of Pentacles, and 2 of Cups. We have covered the Justice card for all things legal (courts, lawyers, certifications, licenses, notary, judges, jury). And the 8 of Pentacles is reading, writing, classes, training, school, documents, and books. The 2 of Cups is agreements and mergers. This combination is talking about a legal agreement being signed. It reads legal, documents, agreed.

Keeping in mind that we are talking about a marriage that is being blocked from a large amount of money, we have to consider that this legal document is a prenuptial agreement. One of the partners is saying that in case of a divorce they will not have claim to certain properties, business, or bank accounts. Seeing in the Thinking position is the 2 of Wands, they seem fine and fully confident with this request.

Back to the cards in the Future positions, they are 8 of Wands for rapid advancement and progress, Page of Wands for announcements (including marriage plans and proposing to someone) and the Strength card. The Strength card can sometimes be hard to interpret. It lends a sense of peace and calm, being undisturbed and trouble free. Therefore, I would see this as the marriage going forward, making the announcement, maybe sending out the invitations (Page of Wands) and no one is disturbed by this. No one objects or makes a fuss. Their marriage is strong and could weather anything. And, it's not about the money because the love they have transcends (Temperance card) everything else.

Will they get their money back?

      The client wanted to know if they were going to get their money back from their credit card company after disputing a charge with a scammer. Obviously, it is always best to know what the reading is for because it narrows the possibilities of the interpretations. She had already talked to a male at the dispute department and he was refusing to honor the refund in favor of the scammer, saying that she hired the man for a service and that he had provided. The amount in dispute was $79.95.

      First is the King of Wands and next is the King of Pentacles. The King of Pentacles would be the credit card company and the King of Wands is the male in the dispute department. In the right column is the 4 of Swords. I would take this to mean that he really doesn't care. It's not his money, after all. He isn't going to lose any sleep over it. In the Environment is the Ace of Pentacles for a significant sum of money. For many people, $79.95 is a lot of money. They have to work many hours to get that to just give it away, much less to a scammer.

In the recent past is the 2 of Pentacles and Page of Cups. The 2 of Pentacles is about balance and exchanges. It can also indicate money being transferred, moved from one place to another. And the Page of Cups is usually a young girl, or a favorite and creative child, a loving and gentle child. But, it can also represent an adult with childlike character who is gentle and trusting. This is going to represent the client. The 2 of Pentacles represents the exchange of money between her and the scammer. These two cards taken out of the context of the dispute could indicate a child fell, tripped, twisted their ankle, or broke a leg. The 2 of Pents doesn't have to be upside to take its reversed meaning of falling. This is true for almost all the cards.

On the cut is the 7 of Swords for criminal intent or activity. The 4 of Pentacles would be the criminal being greedy and wanting the client's money. It means *"mine"* or *"really, really wants it"*. The 5 of Pentacles is the poverty card, or being, ill, injured, rejected or abused. This card could reflect on the client or the scammer. The scammer might think he has to steal because he is poor. Or, he targets the poor because they can't afford to hire an attorney and come after him and he takes advantage of this. If reflecting on the client, then it would say that the theft has left them feeling abused and maybe exasperated their situation of poverty.

In the future positions are 9 of Wands, 7 of Wands, and 2 of Cups. 9 of Wands is the client mounting a defense, she isn't going to just give up on getting her money back. The 7 of Wands shows that her actions will lead to success and the 2 of Cups shows that they come to an agreement. It could be between her and the scammer (doubt it) or the credit card company who refunds her money. In the Thinking position is the 9 of Cups, which means they are happy. We could quickly conclude that they were going to get their money back just because of this card.

House catches fire with total loss.

It is human nature to only want to hear good things. But, tarot is a lot like the news; dramatic things that make bigger ripples in the etheric field are going to be picked up easier than mundane things. Besides, if someone's house is going to catch fire you would like to know about it. A tarot friend of mine saw a house fire in a reading and warned the client. It was winter but the client had recently bought a new heater. Because of the reading, she decided to not turn it on just in case. Within days, that very heater had a recall and someone actually knocked on her door to retrieve it. Because the client took action, the fire didn't happen. The point is that what you see in tarot doesn't have to happen and can be prevented. This is the beauty of tarot.

The first card is the 10 of Pentacles, which represents a home, building, office or room. A person's room could even catch on fire. The next card is the reversed Ace of Wands. A quick look to the right column indicates a disaster and this helps limit the definitions of the Ace of Wands, which is pretty broad. So, you have to think only about the definitions of the card that could relate to a house. These are fires, explosions and electrical problems.

In the Environment is the Knight of Swords. It can represent all types of rescue personnel and vehicles; things like police, ambulance, and fire trucks. In general, it means coming to the rescue with right and noble action. Since we are talking about a fire, this would be police and fire trucks.

In the recent past is the reversed Hermit and Fool. The past positions usually relate to what is happening in the main layout (but it doesn't have to). The reversed Hermit suggests that there is something they didn't see, maybe due to poor lighting, or they didn't check in to it, and the Fool also suggests they aren't aware of it, or ignored something.

In the Future positions are the reversed 7 of Wands for lack of success and failure, and Ace of Pentacles for huge loss of money and destruction of physical property, because the pentacles is the physical world. The reversed Judgement means not being able to recover, not "coming through the fire", so it indicates to me that the fire is a total loss. They will not be able to save anything.

In the cut are the reversed Temperance showing they have been thrown off balance. There would be a lot of stress. It could also mean that things just weren't working out right, sort of like Murphy's law which states that if anything can go wrong, it will. And, the reversed 4 of Swords means they are losing sleep over it, or they don't have a place to sleep. I knew a woman whose house burned and she and her husband had to sleep in their shed for months while they fought the insurance.

The Knight of Pentacles is things like loans, credit cards, or someone offering help. It could be financial help or just helping out in some other way. It could be that they get a loan from the bank or credit union, or they rely on their credit cards until the insurance settles with them.

In the Thinking position is the reversed 6 of Swords. The card means taking a trip. So either they are thinking they don't want to leave or that they don't know where to go. The upright 6 of Swords means moving into smoother waters while leaving troubles behind. You would see ripples in the disturbed waters behind them. Reversed would mean moving into troubled waters because the ripples are now in front of them. So both definitions would be accurate, not wanting to leave or knowing where to go, and moving into trouble waters. Of course, you would want to continue doing more readings, especially trying to find out what could start a fire.

Nephew is stealing from his aunt.

This layout was for me, so I can fill in the details. The first card is the Queen of Cups. This is a nurturing woman. It can also be mother, wife, or water sign (Cancer, Scorpio, and Pisces). I am not a water sign; I am a fire sign, Aries. So why did I get this card? Because, a mother, wife, and nurturing woman can be any sign. I think it mainly represented me in this particular role, and more suited how my nephew saw me.

The second card is the 6 of Pentacles, and shows me doling out the money. I was making good money as a critical care nurse and believed in lifting up the family. What I learned the hard way was that my money was not the solution to other people's problems. And in my nephew's case, he did not want to change the behavior that was causing him all his problems in the first place.

In the right column is the Fool. This card can mean stupid or foolish, being naïve, immature or inexperienced. It can also represent younger people. My nephew was in his early 30's but woefully immature. He still acted like a teenager and wanted to party and have good times. He is an earth sign male, the King of Pentacles, but he doesn't come close to matching the strong earthy energy of that card. Cards for him would represent a child despite his age. If reading for someone I would say, *"This woman is handing out her money and it could be a stupid thing or she is handing it to a younger (immature) person. And it could be both"*.

The Fool card also represents a disabled person, so this could read that she is handing her money to a disabled person. But, we don't have to come to conclusions just yet because there are many more cards to consider in the overall picture. In the Environment is the 7 of Swords. That warns that there is criminal activity happening, like, right now. Or, at least the presence of a criminal in their life. Over the period that my nephew was living with me, this was a consistent card in my own readings. He knows I am a reader and I would tell him about this.

In the Thinking position is the 9 of Swords for tears, emotional or physical pain. There is cause for tears and hurt. In the past are 8 of Swords and Devil card. The 8 of Swords is called the jail card. It shows someone locked up. It means restricted, inhibited, and restrained. The Devil is the drugs card, but can be anything toxic (food, drink, relationships). It means addictions, pot, drugs and alcohol.

I had recently bailed my nephew out of jail for yet another DUI. I paid off his tickets, court costs, previous fines from other DUIs, paid his probation officer, and brought him to live with me with the intention of helping straighten out his life. *I know, I know…*

The 3 card cut has the Knight of Swords, the Knight of Wands, and the Justice card. Knight of Swords are the police. The Knight of Wands shows his trip to jail. It is a card of action, even forced action. You might think it is a stretch to say that it shows someone being taken to jail, but I've actually seen it several times. It can even mean eviction, being forced from your home. The Justice card is all legal aspects of the court house, going before the Judge, his probation officer, and his bail bondsman, even visiting them in jail on visitation days or picking them up from jail.

In the Future positions are the Hermit, reversed Ace of Swords, and 8 of Cups. Something is discovered that causes a big fight, and one or the other leaves. In this case, I discovered that my nephew was stealing cash from me on a regular basis, about $3,000 total, and when he left the house both of us were in tears. He was crying because I was crying. I immediately changed all the locks.

We are doing okay now. I didn't press charges. It was my fault for allowing it to happen in the first place, and no, he never paid me back. He can't afford to. He is married now and raising two teenage girls and working full time.

The baby abused by the babysitter.

    I was reading for a guy at work and had gotten some good information that he later confirmed. For example, I saw a pedestrian getting hit by a vehicle while leaving a club or restaurant. It was on a cut as a side note so I warned him to be careful while driving so that he doesn't hit anyone. It turned out that it was he who got hit by a car while leaving a bar years ago and it had thrown him quite a distance. This was a significant even in his life and he was impressed that it came up.

    Well, after several layouts, the readings changed drastically and the injury of an elder woman or baby started coming through. I asked him to check on his mother; she lived in another state. There was no way I could have known that it was actually talking about my own infant niece. I have learned since then that traumatic information in my own life will bleed through in my readings and you need to be aware of this possibility. It can actually stop you dead in the water and make it almost impossible for you to read for anyone else! I am not even kidding. Within a week, I got the call to come to the hospital. My infant niece had broken ribs. The babysitter had been squeezing her. It was only then that the layouts made sense.

The first card is the Empress for baby or elder. It doesn't have to be the first card down. Next is the 5 of Pentacles for illness or injury. So far, we read that the baby or elder is sick or injured. In the right column is the 7 of Swords, so now we know that this is a deliberate act. In the environment is the reversed 9 of Pentacles meaning they are not in a safe and secured environment. These four cards were consistent and in almost all follow up layouts. Watch for this happening, it means the energy that is causing these cards to be repeatedly pulled is very strong.

In the recent past is the 10 of Wands and Queen of Cups. It shows that this woman, probably the mother has been working very hard. They might even be working on their feet, which she was as a manager of a fast-food restaurant.

In the Thinking position is the reversed 2 of Swords. They are thinking they made a stupid decision. It can also mean they are stuck in making a decision. Of course, the mother was blaming herself for letting this woman babysit her child. She was the wife of her husband's co-worker and they didn't really know her well; a major mistake (also a definition of the Fool card).

The Future contains the 5 of Swords for treacherous acts, which reflects what the babysitter was doing. The 9 of Swords for tears and pain shows the baby crying in pain. And the Knight of Swords shows someone coming to her rescue. The parents took the baby to the ER because she wouldn't stop crying and they didn't know what was wrong. The X-ray showed old and new rib breaks and the police and child protective services were called. There were tense moments while the husband was being threatened with arrest and CPS wanted to take their baby away; a real nightmare.

On the cut, it shows that the family stays together as a unit in the upright 10 of Cups, The Ace of Cups represents the baby and the 4 of Pentacles shows they hang on to the baby. A reversed 10 of Cups would show a broken up family. A reversed 4 of Pentacles would mean they lost possession of the baby.

What happened was that the extended family rallied around the young couple and we talked to the police. Charges were brought against the babysitter but she got off because nothing could be proven. The couple later had a second child and had no more problems with child protective services. This was years ago and the girl is entering High School and making good grades. She wants to be a nurse like her aunt. Back then, I was still new at tarot reading and didn't know what I was looking at. Hopefully this book of layouts is going to put you leaps and bounds ahead in your ability to read tarot.

Breaking new ground in the metaphysical.

There are 7 Major cards in this layout, which indicates something really metaphysical is going on. It is spiritual or divine and from higher realms. This is part of their life path. The first card is the Hierophant. This is the religion card, but not just Christianity even though he represents the Pope. Christianity itself is a conglomerate of many ancient religions, not only monotheistic but pagan as well (there is plenty of information if one chooses). At the core of all religions is man's quest to find God. Next is the High Priestess and she is the source of God's Wisdom, which is the holy spirit, called Shekinah and Sophia. King Solomon dedicated his Temple to her. She is also the "occult", which simply means hidden. She means "private" and "for your eyes only" and "the mysteries", which makes her a card of initiation groups like Masons, Knights Templars, CIA and FBI.

In the right column is the 8 of Pentacles for studying, reading, writing and documents of all sorts. It can be a journal, diary or memoire. These three cards together suggest study into sacred theology and secret mysteries, not just doctrine reserved for the mainstream and "common man".

In the past are the Ace of Cups and Magician. The Ace of Cups can represent having a passion for a thing. The Magician card is about the power of manifestation, and using the source of creation while keeping in line with the laws of creation. You might want to read that again. The laws of creation are God's laws. His antler horns represent our world of nature and the white and black candle represents the duality in nature. He draws upon the source of spiritual potential with his right hand and directs it down to create in the physical world. These cards indicate that they have a strong passion for the spiritual path.

In the Environment is the 6 of Pentacles. They have a good reputation that relates to their spiritual endeavors. They are known in their community and would be respected in this area. There are people who look up to them.

In the Thinking is the Star card. Being without clothes represents a person who is in the spiritual. Her eyes are closed in deep meditation. Water represents mind, the universal mind, of which she has submerged her foot. While in deep meditation, she is at what is called "the threshold of the mind of God", the door in heaven. It is what Christ means when he says in Revelation 3:20 *"Behold, I stand at the door and knock: if any man hears my voice, and opens the door, I will come in to him, and will sup with him, and he with me."* The client has reached the threshold of Divine Unity with the mind of God. This has been the goal of the Great Work of mystics throughout time and there is a body of literature dedicated to it.

In the Future is Hermit, a Mystic, and comes from the word Hermetic, an area definitely worth study. It shows the client upon his spiritual quest. The 8 of Wands means rapid advances, and the Ace of Wands is energetic, magnificent creation and excitement. The client is going to make great gains in their spiritual pursuits.

On the cut are the Fool, Hanged Man, and 4 of Swords. There is no set rule on which direction you read, right to left, left to right or start in the middle. It all depends on how it makes sense to you. 4 of Swords can be meditation, or lying in bed. Hanged Man can be astral travel (by spirit) or remote viewing (by mind), and Fool is new beginnings. Knowing what we already know about the client, I would read this as their mind exploring new ventures while meditating. This could even be the use of the hypnogogic state to delve into the field of information around us. The hypnogogic state has been used by many great men to solve complex problems and by artists to create great works. The hypnogogic state is the moments just before falling asleep and the moments right at awakening. I strongly encourage it.

Don't buy that bad car.

My sister had called me out of the blue from a used car lot. She wanted me to do a reading on a car she was thinking of buying. I grabbed my cards while she was on her cell phone. What I saw was that the car had poor craftsmanship. When she repeated, *"Poor craftsman ship?"* the dealer told her that the car had been made in some odd place, like Korea or Vietnam; which I found alarming.

The first card is Chariot, the vehicle. Next is reversed Ace of Wands (facing right). In relating to vehicles, Ace of Wands refers to the electrical system, so reversed can mean electrical and computer problems. It also means fire and heat. Make real sure the motor is not aluminum because these motors can melt! Reversed Ace of Wands might even mean defects in its "creation". The battery could be corroded because the Ace of Wands can refer to the battery. Spark plugs might be burnt and need replaced because Ace of Wands can be electrical wiring.

In the right column is the Reversed Sun card. This also relates to the vehicle overheating. It can mean leaving it out in the sun, which cracks the dashboard and damages the paint and kills the cells of the battery. The radiator might leak, the thermostat might be stuck. It could have sat near the beach (Sun card) and be damaged by salt water, which rusts the body of the car and ruins brake pads.

In the past is the reversed Ace of Pentacles and since it relates to the physical realm it can be used to represent the physicality and mechanical condition of things. The reversed Magician implies that there is poor craftsmanship, combined with the reversed Ace of Pentacles it reads that poor craftsmanship leads to mechanical problems and affects the functioning of the vehicle.

In the Environment is 5 of Pentacles and represents the car dealer who wanted her to buy the car and was keeping the full truth from her. If you ever see this card in any dealings, stay away!

In the Future positions are the High Priestess and the Page of Wands and relates to the reading itself. It shows the reader, the High Priestess, telling her something (Page of Wands) that results in her walking away from the dealership in the 8 of Pentacles. It is not unusual to see the reading itself show up in the layout.

In the Thinking is the Wheel of Fortune because both of us felt very lucky that she was saved from buying this terrible car. I was glad she had called me. My sister is actually my number one client. I have told her some things she thought impossible and I am always right. She totally trusts my readings.

In the cut is reversed 8 of Wands, the Devil, and reversed Temperance. Reversed 8 of Wands in relation to a vehicle means that the car doesn't have proper momentum. Maybe it acts up at certain speeds. It could be misfiring, the transmission won't shift, or it stalls or has trouble starting. The Devil card shows impurities. There could be dirty oil, it might smoke, there could be water in the gas, or debris in the fuel line. The motor might have oil all over it. The air filter might be dirty (this is important). The car might even be trashed out on the inside.

The reversed Temperance is all types of interference in smooth functioning. It's just not running right. There are many things that would interfere with the car running like it should. There could be a vacuum leak, failing timing belt (change after every 60k miles), broken tie-rod ends, and broken struts or shocks. The alternator or generator might need replaced. If you see the Tower card in relation to a car, suspect it has been wrecked or been in a flood.

Take a moment to consider how much knowing the subject of the reading affects how you read each card.

Great business idea, but beware of documents.

Swords are the element of air and relate to thought. Cups are the element of water and relate to emotions. Pentacles are the element of earth and relate to the physical and Wands are fire and relate to energy. Each Ace card epitomizes the element of that entire suit. So, Ace of Swords is the epitome of thought and represents great intellect, analytical skills, and great ideas. The 3 of Wands is the business card and networking, so with the Ace of Swords indicates making a business based upon a great idea or having a very good business plan or strategy.

The 7 of Wands means success, getting the upper hand, being the leader of the pack. In the Environment is the World card. It can mean that something has come to completion, or they have everything they needed to start this business, having covered all their bases. World also represents interstate, overseas, and flight, so the business could be nationwide, or worldwide. They could be doing business travel, or be a travel agency, or even an airline and booking flights.

In the Thinking is the Queen of Pentacles. It can represent an earth sign woman (Taurus, Virgo, Capricorn) or a darker skinned woman. So, they could be thinking about her. But, it also represents money management or anyone who handles money. They might be an accountant or they are putting together their business financial plan, which would be required for any business loan or grant.

In the Past are the 7 of Cups and Page of Wands. I immediately read this as there having been a misunderstanding about something that was said or that they heard. There may be some false advertising going on because the 7 of Cups could be an illusion that is deliberately made, the situation is cloudy by mistake or intention.

This leads to the Future positions of 5 of Swords, 8 of Pentacles and reversed 2 of Cups. This might have connection with the 7 of Cups and Page of Wands. The 5 of Swords shows a dishonest and untrustworthy person(s) and bad intentions. The 8 of Pentacles is the signing of papers and even though it isn't reversed, *because* it is with the 5 of Swords this makes it highly suspect. There is warning here that there is treachery hiding in the documents and they should not be signed. Someone is trying to steal something, take advantage, or is lying in the documents. Thankfully, the deal does not go through as we see in the reversed 2 of Cups. The agreement is broken.

In the cut is the Death card, the 8 of Cups and the Hermit. The Death card probably relates to the broken agreement because it shows a path being blocked. A blocked path means they have to take another route. The 8 of Cups is a person walking away from something they were already invested in. They had spent energy and emotion in arranging those cups. There is a body of water between them and the cups. The Hermit is research or guidance, a consultant, or contractor. He is someone who gives advice. It is seeking, finding, or investigating. Taking the three cards together, it looks like they ended something and walked away from it. That takes courage. With the Hermit, they will be doing more research or seeking professional advice. To sum it up, it looks like they have a fantastic business idea but had a false start but will continue to pursue it with more research.

Protesting after police encounter.

Protests are not an uncommon these days with cameras recording police interactions in the public. I decided to put together a layout of what a civil unrest might look like. The first card is the 9 of Wands and this is someone in protest. They aren't going to go down without a fight. They are standing up for what they believe in. Next is the Page of Wands which is noise, yelling, screaming, sirens, banging, chanting. It can also be forms of media, being video recorded, Skyped, and Facebook live streamed.

To the right is the 5 of Swords and shows mischief, social disorder, rioting. In the Environment is Tower for destruction and chaos. Because the Tower card is in the environment it tends to place it outside of just you and involves others as well.

In the Thinking is the 5 of Wands for worry and anxiety. There is mental disturbance and maybe conflicts with others. In the Past is the 3 of Swords and 5 of

Cups. 3 of Swords is the most dramatic and severe card in the deck. And with 5 of Cups for grief and loss, it indicates something really terrible has happened. At this point, we don't know what this is. In some cases, it might take several more layouts to find out.

Looking around the layout for clues, there is the cut with 7 of Swords for criminal act and Knight of Swords for police, and reversed Ace of Wands. The Ace of Wands is usually a burst of creative energy. But, the card can be all types of fires and explosions, including gun fire (and fireworks). These three cards can be interpreted as someone committing a criminal act and the police showed up and there was exchange of gunfire. Relating this to the past, the police have killed the person. This incident is behind the civil unrest and protesting.

I am not going to get into whether this was justified or not, this is just a simulated layout to show you what something like this would look like. It could be a reading for what you will be seeing in the news, maybe just for your city.

In the Future are the Emperor, Justice, and the Death card. The Emperor is a very powerful authority figure. It can be any department head, President of a company or even a country, homeland Security, FEMA, District Attorney, Governor, Senator, Chief of police. And the Justice card is the legal system, courts and laws. And the Death card puts an end to something. This can read that an authority figure who is in the legal arena put an end to the protests. Or, an authority figure, who is not in the legal arena but uses the legal system to put an end to the protests. This is an example of how you can combine two cards, "legal authority" or read them separately, "an authority who uses the legal system".

Seeking spiritual wisdom and the mind of God.

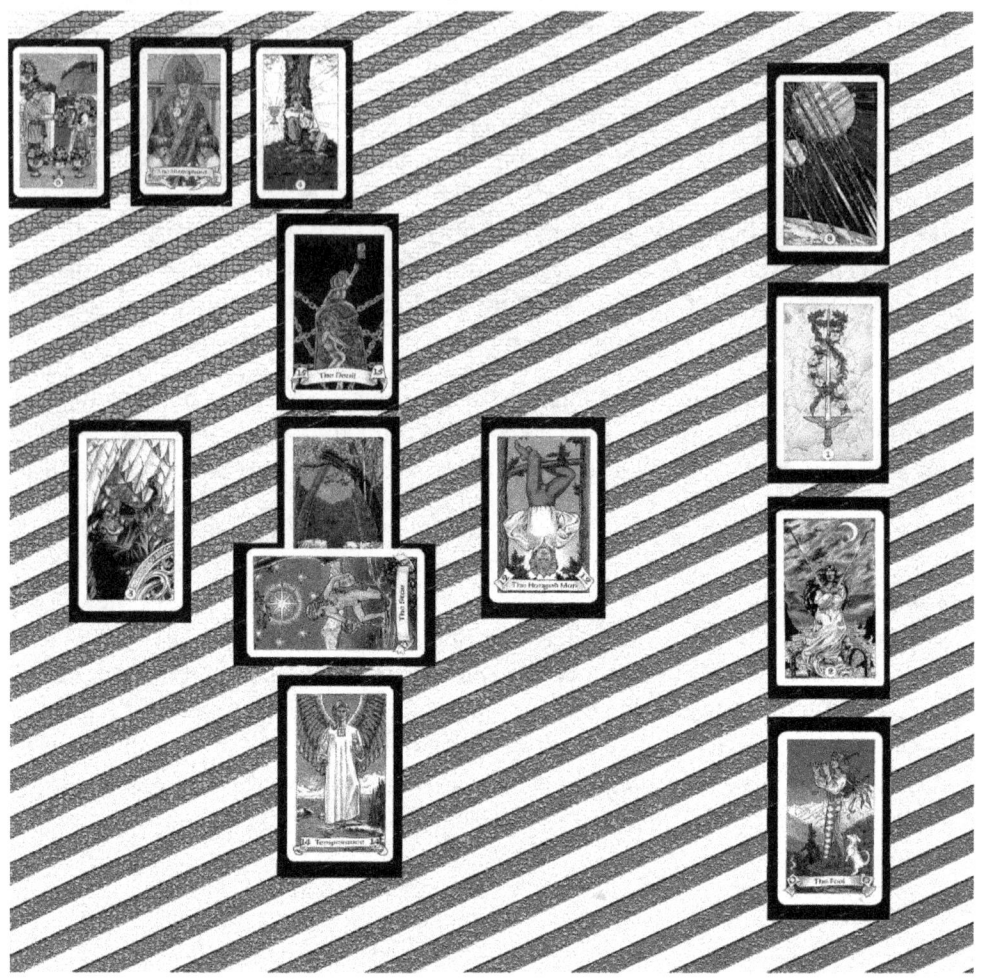

The first thing to notice is that there are 5 Major cards, so something "major" is going on. Therefore, I am going to lean towards their metaphysical representations. I plan a book to look into the possibly of there being ancient Secret Doctrine behind tarot, so watch for that.

The first card is the 4 of swords. The mundane meanings are things like bed, sleeping, relaxing, and even vacation. But the metaphysical meaning is meditation. Next is Star and its meanings are hopes, dreams, and aspirations. But its higher meaning is expanded consciousness, connecting one's mind with the greater mind of the Universe; a kind of cosmic consciousness. To the right is the Fool and his meanings are new beginnings, naïve, innocent, childlike. But its metaphysical meaning is much more profound. He is Ain Soph Aur, the creative force of ALL in the act of differentiating from itself. Meaning, the Fool is that part of God that has chosen to experience itself by separating parts of itself into creation. He represents the very point, at the *beginning*, where God enjoins His spirit into flesh as man. For more on this, please see my tarot articles on Scribd.com.

In the past is the 3 of Pentacles that shows the client working on something of substantial value, notice that he is richly dressed. The Temperance is another profound metaphysical card. Its mundane meaning is balance and flow. The metaphysical meaning represents the Great Work, Magnum Opus, the Philosopher's Stone (Peter). He is the Divine Man. Notice his large stature to his surroundings and that his wings go off the card into the higher realms. These two cards show the client having spent considerable time working on the development of his spiritual self.

In the Environment is the 2 of Swords, a crossroads has been reached, a time of changing directions, or a carefully considered decision. This card indicates a calculated move implied by mathematics in the calipers that she holds.

In the Thinking position is the Ace of Swords. It is the Sword of Light (as in Knights Templar) and represents Spiritual Truth that the client is seeking. In the Future are Devil, Hanged Man and 8 of Wands. Devil is darkness and negativity. But, it is also medications and drugs. We will *suspend* interpreting the Devil card for now, hah, Hanged Man! Another profound card! In Robin Woods version, he is Oden hanging upside down on the Tree of Life, a philosophy also taught in the Kabbalah. It is his body that is in suspension while his mind is set free to merge into the greater mind of the Universe. There are only two ways to do that. One is through transcendental meditation and the other is mind altering drugs. Hence, the Devil card in this instance represents drugs. Ancient mystics and shamans used magic mushrooms and the vine Ayahausca (DMT) to leave their body and travel (8 of Wands) by mind alone. It needs to be warned that Ayahausca is illegal in the U.S. as a Class 1 controlled substance. What we see in these three cards is the client using a drug to travel with their mind alone, leaving the body behind. It gives him the breakthrough (8 Wands) that he has been seeking. Notice that the head of the Hanged Man is illuminated.

On the cut are 6 of Cups for childhood, Hierophant for religion, usually doctrine, and 4 of Cups for disappointed. It reads that they had become disappointed in the religious doctrine of their childhood. This set them upon a quest for something more substantial. They did not want "milk for babies", they wanted "meat for men."

Reading for a cat.

My friend stopped by after a Vet visit with her cat in a carrier. She always covered the carrier with a blanket while in the car to reduce stress. I took the opportunity to do a reading as her cat sniffed around the room. My friend was all for it. The first card is the Chariot for the car trip and the High Priestess. It occurred to me that for the cat, traveling in a car covered with a blanket only to arrive at a totally new location must be a real mystery beyond her comprehension.

To the right is the Queen of Swords for places of healing like hospitals and clinics. For her cat, it was the trip to the Vet. In the Environment is the 8 of Swords and can represent the enclosure of the carrier, a pet cage, or even being fenced in. It can also represent that the pet wants to be free to roam and explore but is being kept locked up in the house.

In the Thinking is the Strength card. This is the card for all types of large and small animals, including insects, right down to germs. It is allergies because people can be allergic to animals. We have to ponder what this card is doing in a cat's thinking position. Was she thinking about another animal; rats, squirrels, birds, fleas?

In the Past is the reversed Hermit for being lost, or feeling lost. The cat might have been a wandering stray. It could have been born feral or escaped from its original owners. The Knight of Swords means coming to the rescue, and shows this cat to be a rescue animal.

In the Future are the 9 of Pentacles, Queen of Cups, and 6 of Cups. The 9 of Pentacles usually means luxury items, property, an enclosed garden and hence security. For a pet, it would be the outdoors.

The Queen of Cups can be the cat's owner, the kind and loving woman. But, it can be its own mother. The 6 of Cups could be the cat's siblings from its litter or the human children in the family. Since there are no children in this cat's home, it must be its siblings. So what then would "outside" have to do with this combination? My friend offered that her cat keeps going to the sliding door to her patio and looking outside as if for something. It occurred to us that the cat thinks its mother and siblings are outside and that if it can just get out the door she would find them. This could relate to the 9 of Swords in the Environment because the cat is trapped in the house and can't get outside where it thinks its mother and siblings are.

On the cut is the 9 of Swords for tears and crying, the 8 of Cups for someone leaving and the 10 of Pentacles for the house. It appears that the cat cries when their owner leaves the house. Or, it at least gets upset about being left behind at the house. Pets sometimes worry that their owner is never going to come back. It takes a while for them to get over this fear.

Past life reading.

It is difficult to read on a past life but some things can be known. All things can be read on, even archaeological sites. In the Past, I have purposely placed both cards that relate to reincarnation. The Judgement card in the Robin Wood deck is the phoenix being reborn from its ashes so represents rebirth and reincarnation. The Magician is also generational, ancestral lineage, heritage and so relates to reincarnation. I show you these cards so that you might consider these definitions in a layout even if you are not specifically looking for a past life connection.

The first card is the 7 of Pentacles for menial labor. He is a blue collar worker, not white collar worker. Next is the Strength card so suggests his work included animals and the Chariot suggests the animals were used as a vehicle. This could be horse and buggy, or using an ox to pull a plow as a farmer. Their work could have related to transporting animals. They could have driven a horse trailer, or pigs to a slaughter house if their past life was more recent. We can limit the definitions of Strength to animals and Chariot to vehicles because we are talking about a person's work.

In the Environment is the 3 of Cups and suggests that food, song, or dance was significant in this life. Did their life include rituals of worship in revelry and merriment? Were they an entertainer? Were they a cook? A farmer?

In the Thinking is reversed Ace of Pentacles. This is money and the material, physical world. They may have lived in constant threat of not having enough. Wealth in an era without currency would be based upon material possessions. For example, having salt was once a measure of one's wealth, or how many sheep or cows that you owned. This means that they weren't a wealthy or royal person in this past life.

In the Future are Fool, 5 of Pentacles, and 3 of Swords. The first card I take into consideration is the 3 of Swords, which is their death. The 5 of Pentacles is injury or illness. You might say, so what, most people die of injury or illness. But things that are not said are as important as what is said. They did not die in battle because we didn't get the Knight of Swords or King of Swords and he wasn't a Knights Templar. He didn't die in old age as shown with the Hermit. He wasn't beheaded as represented by the Hanged Man. He wasn't burned at the stake, as in the Ace of Wands. But, the Ace of Wands is also viruses because it is something alive, so this card would represent all types of plagues (Ebola, Malaria, Black Death, Cholera, or Small Pox). He didn't fall to his death implied by a reversed 2 of Pentacles, and he wasn't poisoned as in the Devil card, and so on.

Now we will consider the Fool card in context to his death by injury or illness. It was an accident, he probably wasn't paying attention. One of the definitions of Fool is being unaware or inexperienced. There was not ill intent, as we would see in the 5 or 7 of Swords. It wasn't punishment as would be implied in the Justice card.

In the cut are the reversed 6 of Swords, the 9 of Wands, and the 4 of Cups. I read this as him not wanting to go somewhere. He is being stubborn in the 9 of Wands and refusing to accept any coaxing, as shown by the 4 of Cups. He seems to be saying, *"I'm not going and you can't make me."* This relates to something of importance that he experienced in this past life or it would not have shown up in this reading. Did it lead in some way to his death; if only he had gone, this accident would not have happened?

The client could examine their life to see if any of these past life incidents are affecting them today. You could do more readings but I don't suggest doing more than five. After that many readings, you should take a break.

Unconventional writing. Retiring.

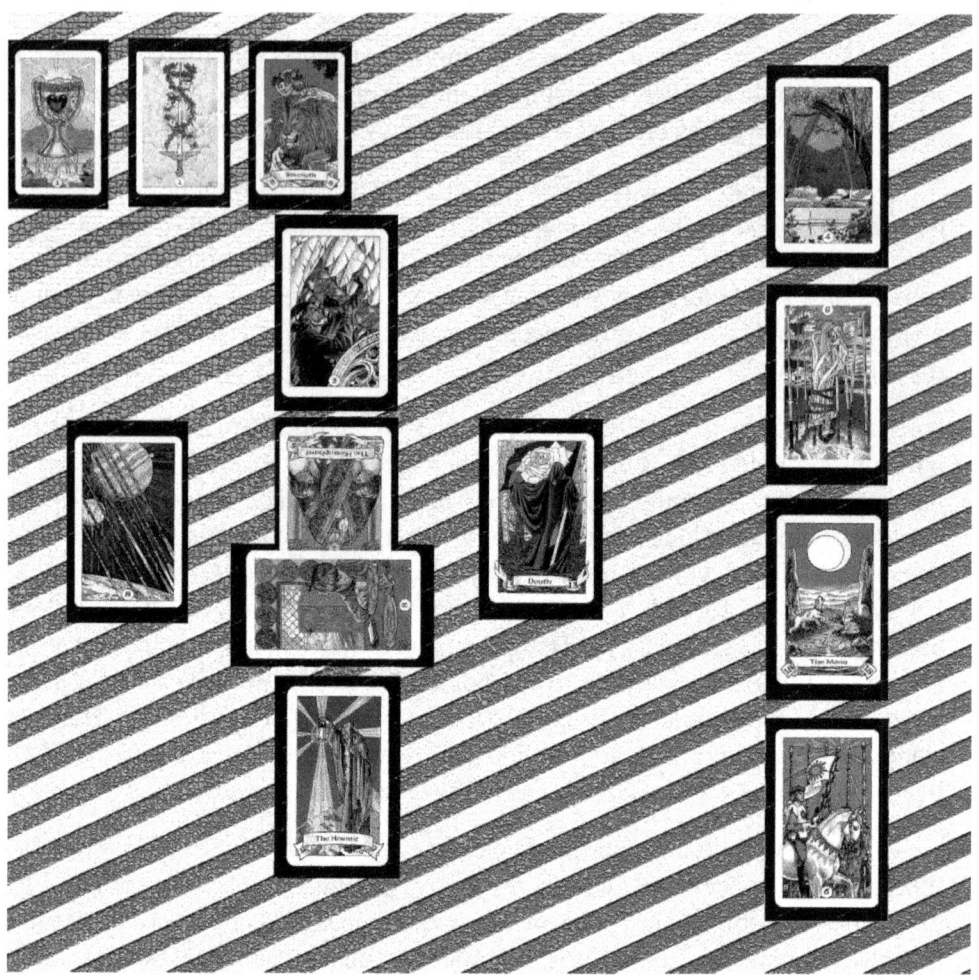

      This layout is based upon a visit to a certified astrologist who read my birth chart and determined what planets were ruling in the heavens for me at that time and going forward. It was very interesting and he was amazingly accurate.

      In the Past is the 8 of Wands. This is the card of astrology and astronomy. The difference is that astrology uses the planets and stars to divine meaning and influence in people's lives. Astronomy is the scientific study of the planets and stars and galaxies. The Hermit represents the guide, the guru, the professional, the counsellor. Together, they can represent a professional in the area of astrology or astronomy. Of course, it can also show getting guidance over a long distance, or a business consultant or therapist that leads to advances and progress. It can be a space traveling satellite that sends back images. It can be a GPS satellite used for coordinates. It can be a Google satellite for mapping the earth's terrain. It is anything traveling in the atmosphere that sees. Stop for a moment to consider these.

The Hierophant reversed means being very non-traditional and unconventional, strange and eccentric. The 8 of pentacles with reversed Hierophant suggests they are reading and writing something on the outer fringes of mainstream. To the right is the 6 of Wands for recognition and appreciation. The astrologer told me based upon the planets that I would be writing things off the beaten path that involved a new paradigm shift and that it would be well received. The definition of "paradigm shift" is when the usual and accepted way of doing or thinking about something changes completely.

In the Environment is the Moon. This is an unusual card. It is the mind, the subconscious, and its deep, dark recesses. It can be a warning to be careful of psychosis, and diseases of the mind. You really don't want it in the "Thinking" position. So, what is it doing here? It can represent being in a more psychic and intuitive phase than usual. But, I was also under a lot of mental stress due to my work in hospice at the time. It can actually represent both, psychic ability and stress.

In the Thinking is the reversed 8 of Swords and it fits perfectly with how I had been feeling. I was burned-out of my job and longed to be free! I would sit on my back deck and beg the universe to free me from my job so that I could focus totally on my research of sacred science and my writings.

In the Future are 3 of Pentacles, Death, and 4 of Swords. The Astrologer saw that a planet in one of my "houses" would bring major focus on my home life. Being able to work from home was a dream of mine. This card combination shows that my job ends and I am at rest physically and mentally. The Astrologer was right. My life now revolves around my home and I am very happy.

On the cut are the Ace of Cups, Ace of Swords, and Strength card. We will take them one by one. The Ace of Cups is love, baby, and passion for a thing. The Ace of Swords is intellect, thought, and strategy. It is the classic Sword of Light, which relates to spirit, which is breath, which is air and thought. The sword is the penetrating power of the mind that cuts through ignorance and wrong thinking to get to the truth, even spiritual truths. So, it becomes the Sword of Truth. The Strength card's higher meaning is about inner calm, peace, and personal power. So, in these three cards we have, *"A passion for spiritual truth that leads to personal power and inner peace"*.

Will candidate #1 win the election? Answer: No.

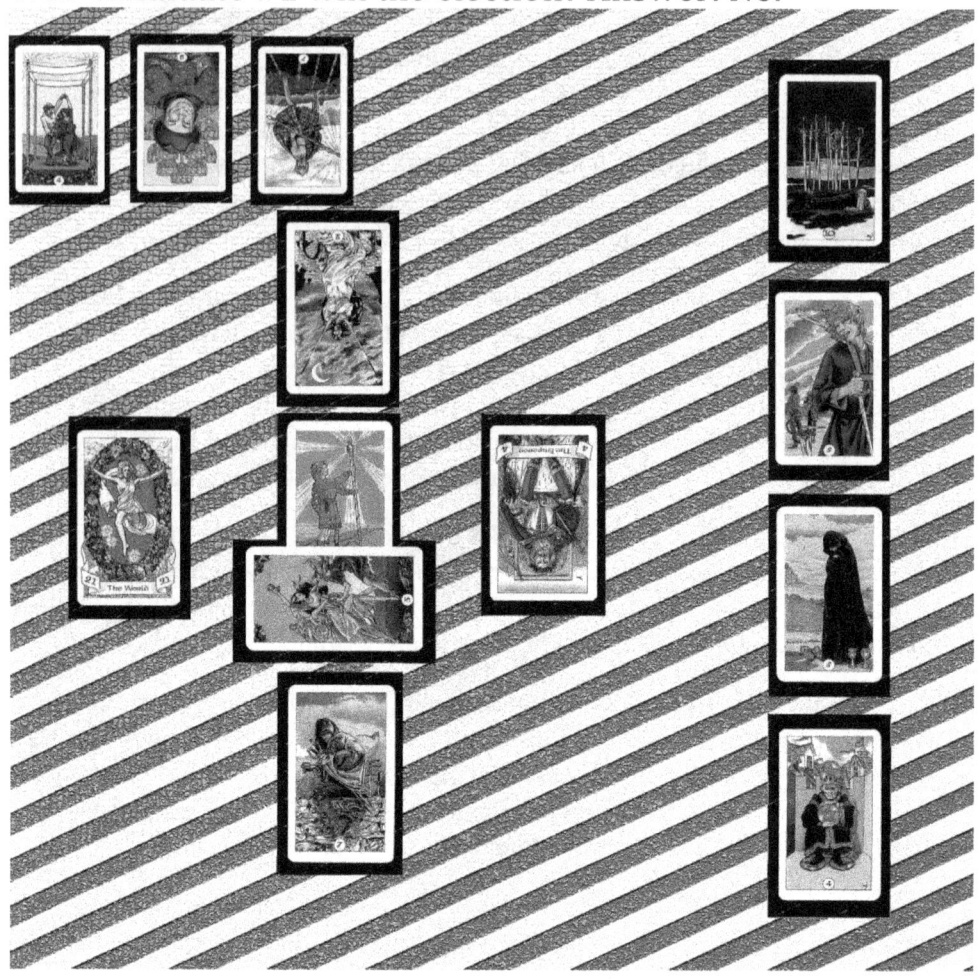

It has become very popular for Tarot readers to read on elections and the political scene. I am going to give you two layouts on elections, one showing a win and the other a defeat. Keep in mind what you are reading for will help you determine what the cards are representing.

First is the Page of Wands. This card represents someone speaking before the public and also represents computers and all forms of media. This includes Television, Facebook, Twitter, Instagram and Skype. One meaning for the 3 of Cups is a lot of people, things like meetings (it can also be a group of women). Together, these two cards read as a speaking engagement or a rally and represents the candidate on their campaign trail. A seminar would look like this. To the right is the 4 of Pentacles and adds the element of covetousness, which is defined as inordinately or wrongly desirous of wealth or possessions; greedy. This drives their speaking out and shows their desire to win.

In the past are the World and 7 of Swords. Wow. By this time in the book, you might recognize what you are seeing in these two cards. Give it a whirl.

Keeping in mind this is a political reading, we will assign the word "global" to the World card. And of course, the 7 of Swords is criminal activity, even covert activity. Let's just go ahead and call it the "conspiracy" card and together we get the term, "global conspiracy". It suggests the presence of a Global Cabal, defined as: *a group of international politicians who meet in secret and are involved in intrigue devoted to world domination.*

In the Environment is the 5 of Swords for grief and loss. It can be the candidate's own but since it is in the environment it more likely represents those in their campaign party and supporters. In the Thinking is the 5 of Swords. Being in the "thinking" position lends an element of paranoia. They think the election was stolen from them by unfair means. People who are crooked expect others to be crooked as well.

In the Future is the reversed 2 of Swords. They are not at all happy with a decision or the direction something has gone in. Politically, the reversed Emperor indicates the overthrow of someone in a seat of power. The 10 of Swords is total devastation and ruin. The Tower card would work here as well. This combination shows they do not win the election.

On the cut is the 4 of Wands, reversed 9 of Cups and reversed 7 of Wands. The deeper meaning of the 4 of Wands is foundation, their base support. Broadly, it means being joined together for a common goal. I left it upright just to mix it up a bit and to remind you that you can take the reversed definitions of any card based upon the cards related to it.

The reversed 9 of Cups is being unhappy. The reversed 7 of Wands means defeat. In the US we currently only have the Democratic and Republican parties. This combination reads that their political party, their base (4 of Wands), is unhappy with the defeat.

Hopefully, by relating these cards with *actual* events it helps you to understand the energies the cards are associated with. The cards in your hands correlate with the energy surrounding an event in the etheric field and by a matter of resonance attracts the corresponding card into the layout. Knowing how this works and focusing with intent helps get a more accurate reading. The process of tarot readings falls under the laws of Physics. It is not "blind reading" and it doesn't require having a "familiar spirit". As spiritual beings we are connected to the whole of the Universe. The cards are simply a tool to acquire, like reading brail, the information found out in the aethers by energy resonance and the laws of attraction (like attracts like).

Will candidate # 2 win the election? Answer: Yes

Here is another example of a political election. The first three cards are at the core of the layout, the crux of it. First is the 6 of Wands, the "celebrity" card. They are well known and in the public eye. They have fans that shower them with accolades. Next is the 2 of Wands and is the card for healthy ego and good self-esteem. They have confidence in their abilities having built upon prior successes. It can even indicate an inflated ego or narcissism, especially if reversed. They are dressed richly and look forward to what the world has to offer.

To the right is the Ace of Swords, the intellect. It also denotes positive energy. As the Sword of Light our candidate could be: a) very intelligent, b) very positive in nature, c) running with a positive platform, or d) they belong to the Knights Templar. Of course, it can be all of the above.

In the Past are the Page of Pentacles and Ace of Pentacles. Page of Pentacles is donations made to their campaign fund, which is legal but has limits. The Ace of Pentacles is a nice sum of money and can be their own money, meaning they are wealthy in their own right. But, Ace of Pentacles could be the larger lump of money compiled by the multiple donations represented by Page of Pentacles.

In the Environment is the Hermit for investigations or getting good counsel. And since it is in the Environment, it represents what is going on around them. Someone could be looking into them, or they are looking into others. It could be hiring the best advisors in their pursuit of the election or their campaign manager. The Hermit would be all agencies that deal in investigations: Homeland Security, FISA, CIA, FBI, TSA, Private Investigators, Spies, and many others.

In the Thinking position is the 9 of Wands. They are not about to back down and are up for a brutal fight. In the Future is Page of Swords for exciting and urgent news. On the Pages shoes are stylized wings, an analogy for Mercury (Hermes), the messenger of the gods. Next is the upright Emperor and means they win the position of power, they are in the sweet seat. Last is the Wheel of Fortune, which represents a big-win.

On the cut are Temperance, Judgement, and 3 of Cups. I placed Temperance because I wanted to cover one of its aspects, being that of a more evolved individual. They are able to make things happen because they work from a higher perspective than most individuals. They are more fully awakened. They may be an initiate of one of the many secret societies which claims to offer enlightenment. This could relate back to the Ace of Swords hinting they are a member of the Knights Templars (or Freemason).

The Judgement card can mean being unscathed by a harrowing experience. Other terms that apply are, *"Coming through the fire"* and *"They came out smelling like a rose"*. The 3 of Cups is a time of celebration. The tinsel falls from the ceiling upon the winner and the crowd goes wild.

Do they really love me?

This is a question many clients have about their relationship. Everybody wants to be loved. The first card is the Knight of Cups and is the romance and suitor card. Water is the element of emotions and this is a watery card. The soft pastel colors of pink and purple also denote love. Next is the Ace of Wands, and it is the embodiment of the element of fire. In romance it indicates strong sexual attraction and heated passion. Robin Wood painted this card as a phallic symbol.

To the right is the 8 of Wands and taken together with the Knight of Cups and Ace of Wands lends the idea of things happening fast because this card is about speed and covering long distance. The saying, *"it was a whirlwind romance"* comes to mind.

In the Environment is the Sun card. The things that come to mind are summer and the beach. This could be a "summer love". Many young romances happen during summer break from school. The Sun card also indicates sunny locations and sunny states. Once, I asked the cards where my sister was and pulled the Sun card in the environment and knew she was at the beach, and indeed she was. The Sun card is also about being very happy and free spirited, like one feels when they are in love.

You may recall that the Sun card is one of several baby cards, such as the Ace of Cups that we see in the Thinking position. Remember, the Thinking position slightly changes how the card is to be interpreted. So, the Ace of Cups might be that they are wondering if this is true love or even if they are pregnant. It doesn't mean they are pregnant, it just means they are thinking about it.

In the Past are reversed Hermit and 4 of Cups. It just means that they were not happy before because they looked for something and couldn't find it. Taking a leap, I am going to suggest that they were looking for love and weren't happy with the current selection out there.

In the Future are Lovers, Page of Wands and 4 of Wands. In a romance reading, Lovers is probably just that and implies sexual relations. In this case it is safe to assume that they are having sex. But, it can just be a couple in a close relationship. If it is imperative that if you must know for sure if they are having sex, turn the card upside down and see if you still pull it.

The Page of Wands is making an announcement. But first, it occurs to me that if we just take these two cards, Lovers and Page of Wands, it can be interpreted in interesting ways. They could be loud during sex. They could be talking about the sex they had. It can mean watching pornography because Page of Wands is multimedia, movies and videos. They might have a Skype channel about sex, or be sending nude images of themselves on their phone. They could be having phone-sex. This is popular with some kids. They could be posting on adult websites, arranging to meet with strangers for a sexual tryst. It can be a dating website, for example a SWM looking for a SWF. Luckily, the 4 of Wands narrows this down so we can scratch off these more racy suggestions.

The 4 of Wand being the wedding card changes the Page of Wands to a proposal of marriage. So, this passionate whirlwind romance is true love that leads to marriage.

Now, let's see what we can make of the cut. We have Star, 2 of Cups, and World. My attention is draw first to the 2 of Cups for friendship, partners, and agreement. The Star is aspirations and having your dream come true. World is about completion and encompassing all. I would say that both partners feel the same way about how much this relationship means to them. They both feel they have found their dream partner, the one that completes them. They don't have to look for love anymore like they were in the past.

Birthdates

Write birthdates on an index card and keep with your deck.

Aries (Fire) - March 21 to April 20

Taurus (Earth) - April 21 to May 20

Gemini (Air) - May 21 to June 20

Cancer (Water) - June 21 to July 22

Leo (Fire) - July 23 to August 22

Virgo (Earth)- August 23 to September 22

Libra (Air) - September 23 to October 23

Scorpio (Water) - October 24 to November 22

Sagittarius (Fire) - November 23 to December 21

Capricorn (Earth) - December 22 to January 19

Aquarius (Air) - January 20 to February 19

Pisces (Water) - February 20 to March 20

King & Queen of Swords: Aquarius. Gemini. Libra.

King & Queen of Pentacles: Virgo. Capricorn. Taurus.

King & Queen of Wands: Aries. Leo. Sagittarius.

King & Queen of Cups: Pisces, Scorpio, Cancer.

Definitions
Major Arcana

0 THE FOOL:. Fidelity. Not cheating. Brand new. Newer or younger. The younger generation. Not experienced or done New beginning. Childlike. Youthful. Naive. Gullible. Unaware. Vulnerable. Trusting. Innocence. Not guilty. A virgin. Pure. Untouched. Unadulterated. Chaste this before. Optimistic. Lack of concern. Lack of foresight. Thoughtless. Unaware of it or knows nothing of it. They are innocent or are found innocent. Oblivious to the fact. Unseen perils. Not enough experience to be wary of dangerous situations.

THE FOOL: (Reversed) Foolish act. Unwise decision. The sensation of feeling stupid or foolish. They feel the other person in question did a stupid thing. A mental or physical disability or mental or physical handicap. Adult with a child's mentality. Mentally slow. Poor or low IQ. They can't read or write. Uneducated. Simpleton. Weak minded. Careless. Easily coerced. Awkward. Clumsy. Crude and uncouth. Many times this card can be upright and still mean its reversed definitions.

1 THE MAGICIAN: An adept. Mastery in their chosen profession or craft. A professional or expert. Skilled. Shows ability. Knowledgeable. Natural. A rugged, earthy man who is virile, potent, charismatic, handsome. A man with a beard. Generational and ancestral lineage and reincarnation. Shaman type person. A naturalist. Herbalist. Learned in natural or holistic healings. Belongs to Hermetic order, Freemasons, or Knights Templar or similar sacred societies.

THE MAGICIAN: (Reversed): Not capable or skilled in their profession or craft. Lacks experience or expertise. Lacks the talent or aptitude. Having self-doubt or feeling inept in their abilities. An object inferior in some way or of poor craftsmanship. Shoddy or sloppy work. Using magic to harm others. Black magic (even if card is upright). Being involved in satanic activity. A hex or curse has been performed.

2 HIGH PRIESTESS: Secret. Hidden information. Private, or personal information. Confidential. Classified. Top secret. Database. Stored information. Mystery. Mystical. Mysterious. Psychic intuition. An individual (male or female) with spiritual gifts of insight and intuition. They may be clairvoyant, clairaudient, or a combination of both. Psychic activity happening. Initiations and secret societies. Spiritual person or teacher. You will get this if reading for another psychic or can show up for the reading or reader them self. She is Isis, the aethers, the quantum field, the Akasha records. She is the unseen creative force in the universe. The magi (Magician) draws upon her to create matter in the physical realm. She is the holy spirit called Shekinah.

HIGH PRIESTESS: (Reversed) Disclosing confidential, private or personal information. Telling a secret. Gossiping. Snitch. Whistle blower. Lacking intuition, insight or knowledge. Self-conscious. Shyness. Is against psychic abilities or practices. Misuse of knowledge, whether they are exposing a secret or hiding something. Wrong use of psychic powers. Psychic attack.

3 THE EMPRESS: Maternity. Pregnancy. A baby. One's mother or mother figure. A matriarch in the family. A wise older female. Elder relatives; grandparents, aunts and uncles. Nurturer or care giver of children or the elderly. Baby sitter. Baby-sitting. Daycare center. Retirement home or nursing home. Medical: Abdominal problems: stomach, gallbladder, pancreas, uterus, other female organs.

THE EMPRESS (reversed): Having a problem with their mother or elders. Difficulty getting pregnant or with the pregnancy. Losing the baby. Miscarriage or abortion. Childless. Being sterile. On birth control pills. Having a hysterectomy. Don't want children or has a fear of parenting. A bad or negligent parent, grandparent, or babysitter. Babysitting problems. Having no parental supervision. A smothering mother. The baby, mother, or an elder is sick. Problems in stomach area or gynecological problems (as upright card).

4 THE EMPEROR: Having a high position (man or woman) or in a position of authority. The owner, boss, or president of a company. Directors and CEOs. Any official organization or department. Human resources. A powerful, virile leader. A President. A dictator. An Official. Having legal authority. Power of attorney. District attorney. Immigration authority or officer. Having dominance over others. A person who's decisions would be purely business and not based on emotion. A stern individual. Bossy, controlling, dominating, aggressive person (even if upright).

THE EMPEROR (Reversed): Stubborn. Dominating. A bully. An obstinate, arrogant and controlling male or female. Lacks emotional concerns. Abuse of power. Loss of a position of power or control over others, or over a situation. Oppressive individual. Lacking restraint in aggression. Being at odds with the established order. Others trying to control you. Dry season. Drought.

5 THE HIEROPHANT: Religious. Place of worship (Church. Temple. Mosque. Synagogue. Monastery. Orphanage, Catholic school). Prayers. God in their life. Spiritual authority (Chaplain. Reverend. Preacher. Minister). A ceremony. A ritual. A thing of tradition. "It's our policy". A traditional institution, department, or organization. Being different. Eccentric. A person of a different color, race, religion, or culture. A homosexual, gay. Foreigner. Alien being.

THE HIEROPHANT (Reversed): Actions that are irregular and go against tradition. They are gay. Feeling shut off from God or that prayers aren't answered. Abandoning a previous belief system or religion. Anti-religious. An atheist. Dogmatic. Fanatical. Hypocrite. Unethical or immoral. A foreign religion or social structure. A couple has social, cultural, racial, or other differences. Person of a different race, religion, or Country. For example, if client is white then the individual in question could be black or Hispanic, If client is black, then individual in question could be white, etc.' An illegal alien. Alien activity as in "aliens".

6 THE LOVERS: A couple who are romantically or sexually involved. Healthy or good relationship and partnership. Well suited for another. Working towards a common goal. Being on the "same page" as another. Equanimity. They complement or balance each other's attributes. A male and a female both. In a health reading represents the reproductive organs including breasts and sex organs. Anything transmitted from person to person whether sexually or not. Even upright can mean sexual abuse.

THE LOVERS (Reversed): The relationship splits up. Having an argument with your partner. It isn't a good relationship. Being mismatched. Growing apart. Unfaithfulness. Cheating. Having an affair with a married or otherwise committed person. A sexually transmitted disease. Any communicable or transmittable, contagious disease regardless of sexual activity. Nudity. Problems with sexual organs (breasts, uterus, penile, prostate). An aberration in sex. Sex addiction. Sexual abuse. Rape. Prostitution. Sexual predator. A pedophile. Impotent. A sex change. A transvestite. Same sex partners.

7 THE CHARIOT: Control. Able to control the direction of a situation. A control issue. A vehicle. At a literal level, the Chariot represents all means of transportation. An automobile. An airplane. A boat. A motorcycle. Even a bicycle, tricycle, scooter, skates, or wheelchair. An actual horse and carriage. Transportation. Trafficking. Metaphysically, having good control of ones ego personality and emotions.

THE CHARIOT (Reversed): Having no control over a situation. It's not in your control. Car problems. Car breaks down. Car is stolen, repossessed or towed. Having no car. Losing control of a vehicle. A crash or wreck of any type of vehicle. Transportation problems.

8 STRENGTH: Having inner strength, fearlessness and courage. Having a calming effect on others. A humanitarian. Peacemaker. Healer. Having a healing touch. Having great empathy and understanding. Perseverance. Leading by a gentle persuasion of feminine energy. Read literally, any animal (wild or domestic). Large animals (horses, cows). Small animals (cats, dogs, rats, birds). Bugs (roaches, fleas, mosquitoes). Having parasites. Having allergies or being allergic. Someone who works with animals. A veterinarian. A animal trainer or groomer. They are afraid.

STRENGTH: (Reversed): Having an infirmity. Feeble. Weak. Malaise. Fatigued. Tired. Fear. Fearful. Afraid. Phobia. Panicked. Panic attacks. Coward. Problem with an animal. Animal abused or injured. An animal attacks. Microbiological agents or organisms; including bacteria, spores, viruses, parasites. Chemical or biological agents. Unable to control things around you. This is one of several cards that can be upright or reversed and represent a problem.

9 THE HERMIT: Having found enlightenment, he or she sheds Light for others. A Counselor. Contract worker or advisor. A leader. A Guide. Seer. Mentor. Guru. Teacher. Giving or receiving guidance. A seeker of truth. Seasoned. Wise person. Therapist or clergy. Spiritual awareness. Looking. Searching for someone or something. A tracker. Bounty hunter. To investigate. Background check. To discover. To expose. Anything used to see, such as glasses, microscope, a light, a telescope. Under surveillance. A surveillance camera. The NSA. A tracking device. GPS device or signal. The 'black box'. Medically: Visual problems. Old age. Senior citizen. Elderly person. Something (anything) that is old or aged (like expired food). Solitude. Reclusive. Isolation. The Winter months.

THE HERMIT (Reversed): Poor advice. Being misled. Being lost or just feeling lost. Unable to find someone or something. A loner. Withdrawn from society. A situation is not investigated. A thing is not or was not visible. Not under surveillance. Not watched. Seeks to hide the truth or is avoiding the truth. Hiding something or some "thing". A hidden agenda. Being kept in 'the dark'. The deceased is not in the Light. Losing one's spiritual way. Problems with lighting or being able to see. Vision or eye problems. Cataracts. Needs glasses. Blindness. Eye injury, eye infections or lazy eye. Nighttime.

10 WHEEL OF FORTUNE: Good fortune. Good luck. Lucky for you or in your favor. An inheritance. The situation turns around for the better. Winning. Gambling. Lottery. Some action you have taken will bring good fortune. Making lots of money. A windfall. Summer months.

WHEEL OF FORTUNE (Reversed): A reversal of fortune. Things are not in your favor. Being unlucky. Misfortune. Losing the gamble. Bankruptcy. Not getting the inheritance. Winter months.

11 JUSTICE: The legal system. Legal matters. Legal authority. Any governmental department or office. Court systems (criminal, juvenile, child protective). Fairness. Balance. Justice. Action is justified. Right decision. Equality. Unbiased. Doing the right thing. Rational thought. Negotiations. Anything legal; certification, licensing, tests, contracts. Discerning the truth. A specific technology. Science. Research. They are in politics. Legal professions: lawyer, Judge, jury, mediator, bail bondsman. School testing or medical testing.

JUSTICE (Reversed): Legal problems. Having the judgment go against them. Being sued. Delays in legal matters. Being penalized. Losing your license or certification. Licensing or certificates revoked. Failing a test. Not passing the boards. Discrimination. An injustice done. Treated unfairly. Biased. Showing prejudice. Harassment. It is not legal. Incrimination. Dirty politics.

12 THE HANGED MAN: In limbo. Things are on pause. Suspended physically. Delays. Postponing gratification. Sacrifice for others or for a higher good. Betting suspended such as from work or school. Seeking truth or inner vision. Piercing the veil. Raising one's consciousness. Having visions. Remote viewing. Meditation. An inter-dimensional Being. Astral travel, OBE. Being visited by a spirit. Having a spirit attachment. Presence of a disembodied consciousness. An entity. Alien activity. Depending on surrounding cards, can mean a serious situation, accident or injury that threatens life. Life hangs in the balance. Incapacitated. Problems or injury iin head, neck, or throat areas. Hung. Choked. Suffocated. Strangled. Beheaded. Drowned. Something that bites or stings. A bee, snake or spider.

THE HANGED MAN (Reversed): The reversed is much like the upright. Choking. Strangled. Suffocating. Vomiting and aspirating. Drowning. Read literally: Death by hanging. Beheaded. Negative influences of a spirit attachment. Sacrificing one's life or own dreams for the benefit of others. Problem or injury in the head, neck, or throat areas. A major injury or trauma. Someone who is very ill and suffering. Their life hangs by a thread; it could go either way. Almost as ominous as the 3 of Swords.

13 DEATH: Dramatic change. The original path is blocked and one is forced to take a different path. A profound transition or transformation. The end of one era and the beginning of another. Pursuing a dead end. Something is finished. Final. The end. It's over. The death of a career, business, or relationship. The action or activity is being blocked. Rarely means actual death unless surrounding cards support such a scenario. The presence or message from a dead person. Medically: Menopause. Necrosis (decay). Gangrene.

DEATH (Reversed): Staying in a situation they should not. Continuing down the wrong path. Resistance to change. Stuck in old habits. Stagnation. In a rut. Gotten all they can out of a situation. No growth occurring. No changes made. Going into remission. Something going on for a very long time (good or bad). Death will not occur as feared. Can indicate that a person is not actually dead. They survived a near death experience. Does not recognize they are dead. Medically: the word 'chronic'. In a dormant state. Is in remission.

14 TEMPERANCE: Balance. Stability. Organized. Coordination. Synchronizing. Patience. A thing being in a process. Running smoothly. Transformation. Manifesting. In due time (the wheels are turning). Bringing things to pass. They can do anything. They can make things happen. Having flow. Doing the right thing at the right time. Functioning from their higher self. Being highly evolved spiritually. Working with the higher realms and angels. Divine intervention or protection. One's Spirit guide or Guardian Angel. The object in question is made of metal. Metallurgy (gold, silver, copper).

TEMPERANCE (Reversed): Unable to cope. Feeling overwhelmed with the situation. Stressed and burnt out. Feeling off balanced. A thing out of balance. Uncoordinated. Impatient. Lack of flow. Working against the Light.

15 THE DEVIL: Obsession. Compulsion. Greed and corruption. Drug addiction (prescription or not). Perversion of desire, lust, appetite, excess. Obsessive-compulsive behaviors or habits. Of a negative influence. Negative energy or entity. The dark side. Anything bad for you: drugs, alcohol, caffeine, smoking, overeating, sexual deviations. Abusive or harmful relationships. Anything toxic for you. Actual toxins (chemical, gases, poison, pollutants, pesticides, rotten, contaminated purulent, infected).

THE DEVIL (Reversed): Breaking free from a drug or alcohol addiction, an obsession, or a bad habit. Releasing oneself from any negative situation or toxic relationship. Letting go of attachment to material possessions or of negative emotions. Freeing oneself from an evil influence. Working against dark energies: light Worker, Reiki, healing touch. Clearing negative energy.

16 THE TOWER: Ruin and devastation. Disaster. Catastrophic event. Chaos. Swift and dramatic event. Violent weather such as represented in the card (earthquake, lightning, flood, tornado, fires, drought, hurricane, mud slide, typhoon, tsunami). Forces beyond one's control. Broken relationships. Loss of property. Bankrupt. Disgrace. Loss of one's status in life. A great investment of time and effort now crumbles to ruins. Having a major crisis. Beware if you are seeing this card in several client's readings and your own. It could foretell of a disaster to occur, either locally or of a global consequences; especially if in the environment position.

THE TOWER (Reversed): Narrowly escaping a disaster. A crisis is averted. A crisis is now over. Having come through a harrowing time. A lesser devastation or lesser dramatic event than could have occurred. Having missed being involved in a severe weather situation. What was once a disaster isn't such a disaster any longer or a bad situation is reversed.

17 THE STAR: Hopes and wishes. Aspirations and dreams. Bright prospects. Spiritual growth. Achieving a cherished goal. Attainment. Obtaining what they want in life. An astrologer or astronomer. Something from the sky. Not of this world. The alien abductee card (so is Hierophant card). Spring time. Nighttime.

STAR: (Reversed): Dashed hopes and dreams. Not achieving one's goals or desires. Unsuccessful. Let down or disappointment. An expectation went unfulfilled. Lack of inspiration or motivation. Lost all hope or promise. An end of their career. Something falls or "comes down from" the sky. Asteroid or Meteorite. Plane crash. UFO.

18 THE MOON: The subconscious mind. Psychic activity. Could mean to trust your instincts and intuition. Confused as how to proceed. Because of the moon's magnetic pull, which affects the tides, it also affects us mentally so indicates a multitude of mental disturbances, breakdowns and psychosis. Feeling restless. Mental strain. Mentally unstable. Scattered thought. Unable to concentrate. Memory loss. ADHD. Sundowners. TIA's, Amnesia. Dementia. Alzheimer's. Being unconscious. Coma. The moon's glow is just a reflection and hence the traditional meaning of a warning of illusion and deception. The actual moon. Medically it represents anything round; tumors, cysts, growths, etc.' Nighttime.

MOON (Reversed): All upright definitions but worse. Mentally disturbed. Things aren't what they seem. Misperceiving. Mental disorders. Stroke. Psychotic break or episode. Paranoia. Schizophrenia. Hallucinations.

19 THE SUN: Happiness. Jubilation. Enthusiasm. A sense of freedom and feeling uninhibited. Contentment. Having no troubles. The birth of a child. Pregnant. A baby. Could mean it is their birthday. Having a bright, sunny personality. Feeling young and vibrant. Playing in the sun. At the beach. Taking vacation at a sunny location. Sunbathing. Indicates temperatures and extremes of heat. Summer months. Daytime.

THE SUN (Reversed): Being unhappy. Depression. Having an unpleasant, disagreeable disposition. Getting too hot. Sun-stroke. Sun burned. Fever. Dehydration. Drought. A thing gets over heated. Seasonal Affective Disorder (SAD). Winter months. Sometimes, getting this card upright can still mean its reversed definition of depression. Always consider a card's reversed meaning as being a possibility.

20 JUDGEMENT: Attainment. Great success. Victory. Realization. Triumphant. Overcoming adversity. Coming through a time of tribulation (i.e. 'through the fire'). Absolution (vindicated) and redemption. Being in good physical health. Physically fit. Good stamina. A trim or muscular body (the 6-pak abs). Being revitalized, re-energized. Getting physical therapy, a chiropractor, acupuncture. Purified and cleansed. Regaining one's health. Making a full recovery. Anything to do with the physical body. Dance. Yoga. The gym. Exercising. The naked body. A stripper. A thing has been refurbished and is like new. Rejuvenation and rebirth. Reincarnation.

JUDGEMENT (Reversed): Poor health. Does not recover or regain one's health. Is not rejuvenated. Physically unfit. Body (or item) is in poor condition. Feeling run down and tired. Unable to be restored to its original form and function.

21 THE WORLD: Completion. Encompassing all. The whole. Attainment of desire. Self-actualization. Reached a major goal. The ultimate (of anything). An epitome. Triumphant. Limitless. Infinite. Universal or world-wide. International. A multinational. Indicates another State or city. Transcontinental flight. Overseas or Interstate travel. From another Country. A collective whole (everyone, everything). Not earthbound. Anything above the earth. Airplane. Drone. Satellite. Space shuttle. UFO. Circles the earth. Upper atmosphere. The end of the journey begun by the Fool. As a health card: their circulation. In the case of cancer, means metastasized.

THE WORLD (Reversed): Feeling incomplete or unfulfilled. A thing or act is not completed. Having not reached their goals. It ain't over (in regards to a relationship or situation). Falls to earth. Down from above. Losing altitude. Flight problems or delays. No interstate travel is allowed (for legal reasons). Airplane crash. The soul is earthbound.

BLANK CARD: Not all decks have a blank card. If this card appears in the future it indicates that the outcome is flexible and can be changed, or is yet undetermined. If it appears in the past, the person cannot remember what happened in the past, or that something has been erased. Expunged. If it falls in the present, the options are open or flexible. If the first card down, they have not thought about the issues presented in the layout yet. This card also means starting with a clean slate. Not knowing. Empty. Blank. Deleted. Destroyed. Clean. Sterile. It was removed. Disappeared. Not there. It never happened. It didn't or won't occur. Destruction of evidence. Having no clues. Having no evidence. They do not know anything about it. Having no plans. Clear conscious. If your deck didn't come with a blank card, you can make one by gluing a blank paper to any extra card that came with the deck.

Before we proceed, it should be said that sometimes not getting an expected card in the layout is just as significant. For example, they want to know if their lover is cheating but you don't get a 7 of Swords, or a reversed Lovers card, or a reversed Knight of Cups, etc.' In this case, you would say, *"I don't see anything that indicates that they are cheating"*.

Another thing to point out is that there is no hard and fast rule that you have to take the upright definition of a card if it falls upright. The better way to read is to be flexible while going through a type of mental gymnastics as you consider surrounding cards to determine which definitions might apply. You will find that learning tarot improves your mental agility and problem solving skills in your everyday life.

Swords

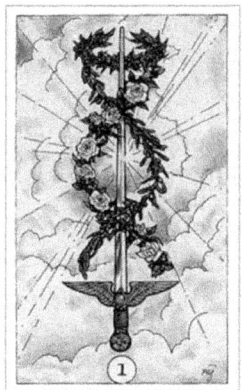

ACE OF SWORDS: Success. Victory. Attainment. Knowledge. Technology. The answer is yes. Absolutely. Positively. Positive attitude. Positive thinking. Inspirational. A good outcome to any endeavor. Clarity of thought. Sharp mind. Intelligent. Analytical process. Strategic. Brilliant. Very bright. Read literally, any sharp object or sharp pain. Swords mean knowledge but also encompass the whole of war and peace. They are in the Light. Positive energy (white Light). Spiritual.

ACE OF SWORDS (Reversed): Negative thinking. Negative attitude. Over judgmental. Criticizing. Faultfinding. Nitpicker. Contradicting person. Discouraging individual. Confrontational. A hostile person, environment, or situation. Mental frustration and tension. Over thinking. Over analyzing. A poor strategist. Big fight. Declaration of war! The reversed Ace of Swords came up for the event of 911.

2 OF SWORDS: Decision. A choice between two things or actions. Careful consideration. Setting priorities. The number 2 is the number of duality, balance, and choice. An important choice or decision has to be made. This card is about personal changes or it was (or is) a crossroads in their life. Things have changed. Changes were made (to it). Took it in a different direction.

2 OF SWORDS (Reversed): Making a wrong choice or wrong decision. Cannot choose or refusing to choose or make a decision. Not knowing how to proceed or address an issue. It is not their choice or decision to make.

 3 OF SWORDS: Tragedy! Serious injury or accident. Sudden illness. Death. Murder. Suicide. Hatred. Kill. Die. Shot. Stabbed. Cut. Bleeding. Divorce! Separated from. Severance. Fired! Quitting! Heartbreak. Emotional pain. Heart attack. Heart surgery. Severed artery. Stroke. Hemorrhage. Any surgery. Needle stick. IV drug user. Tattoos. The definitions this card could cover are almost endless, anything that cuts, punctures, pierces, or causes physical injury. This is the most dramatic card and means death more often than the death card. It is highly recommended that if you get this card that you pursue it so that the event might be avoided, and it very well can be.

3 OF SWORDS (Reversed): Still serious but less dramatic when reversed. Does not commit suicide or murder. Does not die. Is not killed. Heartbreaks, injuries, and surgeries are less severe. Having a crisis intervention.

There are 5 cards that if seen together in a reading can indicate actual death. The 3 of swords, 5 of cups (grief), 9 of swords (tears), Tower card, and least of all, the death card. The death card is not about death but about endings and transformations. At least 3 of these should be present to even suggest a death. Unfortunately, the 3 of swords alone can mean death, serious life threatening accident or surgery. But if also present with death card is the 5 of cups or 9 of swords, or tower card, then death is much more likely and should at least be gently presented as a possibility. Many just want to hear good things, but if you don't mention it and something does occur they will question why you didn't catch it. You could start by asking, *"If I see something bad, would you want me to tell you about it?"*

4 OF SWORDS: At rest. Relaxation. Recuperation. Recovery time. Vacation. Time off. A leave of absence. A period of introspection. Meditation. Hypnosis. Being on bed rest (as during pregnancy). Bedridden. Sleep. A bed. A bedroom. Being at peace. Having peace of mind. Taking it easy. Not working. Just being lazy. "No sweat". It doesn't bother them in the least.

4 OF SWORDS (Reversed): Not getting enough rest or sleep. Sleeping too much. Sleep disorders. Insomnia. Sleep apnea. Narcolepsy. Not resting well or not feeling rejuvenated. Feeling tired. Drowsy. Lethargic. No free time. Needs a vacation or a break. Vacation is interrupted or postponed. Doesn't have a bed. No place to sleep.

5 OF SWORDS: Trouble. Difficulties. Cheater! Trickery. Sneaky. Sly. Deceit. Liar! Stealing. Treachery. Deception. Betrayal. A ruse. A gimmick. An imposter. Phishing. A scheme. Taking advantage of others. Winning by unfair means. Gossip. Mocking. 'Back stabbing'. Watch your back. Taking another's credit for something that is not theirs. Deliberate effort to defeat or do harm to an endeavor. Undermining a project. Picked on. Bullying.

5 OF SWORDS (Reversed): They are trying to take advantage of another but aren't getting anywhere. Thwarting or diverting an attempt by another to do harm.

6 OF SWORDS: Taking a trip by road, plane, or over water. Someone journeys to see you or you to see them. Being from out of State. Leaving troubles behind. Situation improves. Tensions ease. Their destiny. An actual boat or ship.

6 OF SWORDS (Reversed): Trip canceled or delayed. Having to take a trip that is objectionable or that one loathes to take. Something has gone wrong with the trip. Actions are taking you into troubled waters. Losing the trail. Thrown off the track. Going the wrong way. Read literally, going back the way they came. They return or circle back. Upright

or reversed, someone may be scoping out your house or work such as doing drive-by's to check it out. Look for other trouble cards.

7 OF SWORDS: A criminal. Criminal activity. Illegal. An illegal alien.

Stealing. Robbery. Intruder. Infiltrator. Treachery. Betrayal. Sabotage. Malice intent. Conspiracy. Kidnapping. Being stalked. Fraud. Stolen identity. "Cat-Phishing". Extortion. Adultery. They are cheating. Drug dealing. Spying. Private investigator. A spy or double agent. Cunning. They are guilty. Being paranoid. Being secretive. Being suspicious. Covers all negative human emotions and actions. Covers all criminal activity and any covert governmental activity.

7 OF SWORDS (Reversed): Same as upright meaning but adds the element of deception and subterfuge, not an "in your face" kind of criminal. It's a gimmick or scam. Ponzi scheme. Double-dealing. 'Cooking the books'. An imposter. A ruse. A trick. Being fleeced. Being 'taken-in' or being manipulated. A habitual criminal. A career criminal. A predator. A stalker.

8 OF SWORDS: Trapped. Restricted. Hindered. Prohibited. Restrained. Restraining order. Inhibitions. Committed. Obligated. The prison or jail card. Someone will be going to jail or is in jail. Detained. Child grounded. Locked in. Fear of commitment. Loss of freedom or free time. Inaction through fear. Read literally, tied up. Kidnapped. Captive. Forced. For pets; a cage, their carrier, collar, or harness. A fence. Indicates a soul is earthbound.

8 OF SWORDS (Reversed): Freedom! Escaping. Untied. Unrestrained. Loose. Released from jail. Refuses to be tied down or obligated to a job, project or relationship. Free from inhibitions. Medically: Respiratory ailments. COPD. Emphysema. Asthma. Pulmonary fibrosis. Lung cancer, especially if with Knight of Swords (cancer). Congested. Chronic cough. Bronchitis. The flu. Broken rib. Crushed chest. The soul is free from the physical body. The soul is not earthbound.

9 OF SWORDS: Tears. Crying. Feeling hurt. Emotional upset. Mental anguish. Troubles and woe. Reliving past injuries. Actual physical pain. Fibromyalgia (pain syndrome). Nightmares. Bad dreams. Night terrors.

9 OF SWORDS (Reversed): Coming through a time of emotional pain or physical suffering. Getting pain relief. No more crying. Anguish is over. Having mentally worked through issues that were once causing distress and heartache. It wasn't painful, or was not in pain.

10 OF SWORDS: Devastated! Totally ruined. Major betrayal. Stabbed in the back. Victimized. Martyrdom. Completely drained and depleted of all energy, or motivation. Drained of their resources. Feeling exhausted. Letting others exhaust your time and energy. Medical: Bleeding out. Free bleeder. Bled to death. Anemia. Ruptured spleen. Broken back. Vertebrae problems. Ruptured discs. Metal plates, shrapnel, or pins in the back. Prosthetics. Heavy metals in the body: mercury, lead, nickel..

10 OF SWORDS (Reversed): Overcoming devastation. Refusing to be victimized or taken advantage of anymore. Resentment of prior mistreatment. Using your energies and resources wisely. Bone, back, or vertebra problems.

PAGE OF SWORDS: Urgent, exciting, or alarming and unexpected news! A sense of urgency. Hearing of problems and difficulties, maybe even learning about it on the news or in newspapers. Unconventional (risky or dangerous) activity. Swiftness. All of a sudden. A very active, alert, fast moving, intelligent child. Hyperactive behavior. A youth (male or female) born in air sign (Aquarius, Libra, Gemini). A young soldier. A youth with a weapon. A male child if question is of gender (even though all Pages in this deck are girls).

PAGE OF SWORDS (Reversed): Behavioral problems in a child (or an immature adult). They are irrational, undisciplined. Their behavior is out of control. They are impatient, inconsistent, unpredictable, possibly even hostile. Hyperactive child. An errant, wayward troubled child.

KNIGHT OF SWORDS: Heroic. Coming to the rescue. Police officer. Fire fighter. Security guard. Ranger. Medical emergency personnel or paramedic. FEMA. Red Cross. Defender of truth and justice. Righteous anger. Noble action. Armed. Carries a weapon for use in their profession. Mounting a defense. An attack. Many times this card takes its reversed definition even though it is upright.

KNIGHT OF SWORDS (Reversed): Very angry! Violent action. Weaponry. Guns or knives. Unregistered or illegal firearms. Radical behavior. Dishonorable. Dishonesty. Can mean a lack of courage. Since anger is said to manifest in our body as cancer, as a medical card this can indicate the presence of cancer.

QUEEN OF SWORDS: Air sign female (Aquarius, Gemini, Libra). Healer. Nurse, Energy worker. Reiki. Chiropractor. Female doctor. Teacher. A female soldier. Confident and strong woman. She has known pain and loss and become stronger from it. She offers healing to others. Any place that you go for healing. A clinic. A hospital. A spa. For pet readings, a veterinarian.

QUEEN OF SWORDS (Reversed): Unable to move forward past (his or her) own personal pain. Feelings are hurt. Feeling insulted. Wallowing in past injustices. Unwilling to forgive or forget. Bitterness. Controlling. Mistrust of others. Cold-hearted. Cruel. Hurtful. Sharp-tongued. Mean spirited. A single woman. Divorced or widowed woman.

KING OF SWORDS: Air sign male (Aquarius, Libra, Gemini). A soldier. A military leader. Serious and analytical (male or female). Strong-willed. Intelligent and independent. Perceptive. Someone involved in mental work. Researcher. Attorney. Lawyer. Counselor. Professor. Troubleshooter. He carries a tool or weapon in his profession. Surgeon. This card will usually be a real person rather than a situation.

KING OF SWORDS (Reversed): Terrorist. Neurotic. Grumpy. Grouch. Overbearing. Uses words to wound. Cruel. Cynical. Mocking. Fixed in his or her opinions. Difficult to deal with. Intense. Cold-hearted. Can be a domineering older woman. The military enemy. Could have a weapon and mean they are armed and dangerous. These negative qualities can represent male or female.

Cups

ACE OF CUPS: True love. Compassion. Passion for something. Being loved up on. Altruism. Sincerity. In good faith. Dedicated and loyal. Pregnancy (beating heart in a womb). Fertility. Birth of a child. Abundance (cup runneth over). Cups are the symbol of water, emotions, womb, feminine intuition, unconscious mind, being receptive (a vessel).

ACE OF CUPS (Reversed): Missing their loved one. Lost their love. Love spurned (rejected). Feeling empty and alone. Disappointment in love. Withholding their love. They are not in love. Never felt loved. Feeling unwanted or unloved. Lacking passion or desire for a thing, a person, or for sex. An unwanted pregnancy. Medical: Dehydration or fluid overload. Congestive heart failure.

2 OF CUPS: In agreement. Partnership. Relationship. Friendship. Best friends. Engaged. Merger. Mutual. Cooperation. Collaboration. Mentoring. Reciprocal. Reconciliation. Making arrangements. Sharing. Being supportive. Conception. Twins. Cell phone. Satellite. The number 2.

2 OF CUPS (Reversed): Broken friendships or relationships. Breaking or not honoring the agreement. Not making an agreement. Non reconciliation. Does not approve. Not cooperating. Rejects the proposal. A big quarrel. A falling out. Problem with the mentorship. Medically: Problem with the kidneys (renal).

3 OF CUPS: Celebration. Holiday. Party. Dancing. Socializing. A gathering. A meeting. Ceremony. Merriment. Many people involved. A women's group or women's club. Women in general. Family reunion, or gathering. Any occasion where people are together. Food or drink. Alcohol is involved. The kitchen. A club or restaurant. Works with food: waitress, cook, or chef.

3 OF CUPS (Reversed): Celebration turned to disappointment. An unhappy occasion, such as a funeral. A meeting goes bad. Wants to party all the time. Problem with food and drink such as contamination, bacteria, toxicity, poisoning. Partaking in too much food or alcohol. Gluttony. Fasting. Having no food. Hungry. Starving. Famine. Medically: Diabetic. Alcoholic. Food allergies. Malnutrition. Anorexia. Bulimia.

4 OF CUPS: Discontented. Not satisfied. Disappointed. Disinterested. Withdrawal. Melancholy. Apathy. Unmotivated. Laziness. Couldn't care less. Unfulfilled. Stubborn. Hard-headed. Not knowing what one wants. Brooding. Moody. Pessimistic. Melancholy. Despondent. A negative person. A 'downer". A naysayer. No fun to be around. Being a "wet blanket". Lacks enthusiasm or passion. Lacks attention or focus. Their glass is always half empty. Rejecting help offered.

4 OF CUPS (Reversed): Motivated. Determined. Made up their mind. Uncompromising. Unwavering. Focused. Deliberate. Conviction in opinion or action. Unshakable. Bring on hyper-alert. Noticing everything.

5 OF CUPS: Grief, loss, and despair. Sorrow. Regrets. Mourning. Grieving. Misery. Great disappointment. Disillusioned. Medically: Blood loss. Anemia.

5 OF CUPS (Reversed): Recovering emotionally from grief and loss. There are no regrets. They are not grieving. The reason for feeling sorrow is over with. Starting anew. A clean slate. Recovering what you lost.

6 OF CUPS: Children. Kids. Brothers and sisters. Cousins. Nieces and nephews. A group of kids. A place where there are lots of children; schools, colleges, daycare's. Pets that are loved and treated as children. Their childhood. The root of a situation is from their childhood. They know this person from their childhood.

6 OF CUP (Reversed): Problem with the children. Juvenile delinquents. Gang member. A gang of kids. A run away. Trouble with your siblings. They lost a child to a death or in a custody battle. A sickly child. Homeless children. They are childless. Could indicate that they do not like the children, or don't like kids, period! A troubled and unhappy childhood. Abused or neglected children.

7 OF CUPS: Imagination. Wondering. Daydreaming. Fantasy. Infatuation. Illusion. Delusional. Unrealistic. It's all in their head. Irrational. Visualizing. Having visions. A dream. Many choices. A speculation. Muddled. Faking it. It's fake. Faux. A facsimile. Counterfeit. Costume. Make believe. A play. Actresses and Actors. Represents all entertainment, arts and crafting. Pictures. Paintings. A painter. Artist. Photographer. Musician. Decorator. Auditory or visual hallucinations. A misunderstanding. Read literally: smoke, dust, fog, fumes, odors, heavy smoker, ash (same for reversed). This card repeatedly came up for the Russian fires of July/August 2010.

7 OF CUPS (Reversed): Misunderstanding. Misconceptions. Misinterpreting. Twisting reality to fit one's needs. Unable to discern between reality and illusion. Imagination running wild. Living in a fantasy world. Not what it appears to be. An illusion. Deceptive appearance. A disguise or it is disguised. Mistaken identity. False or stolen identity. Identity crisis. Bad dreams. Nightmares. Heavy smoker. Something wrong with the air. Unable to breathe. Toxic air. Fumes. Foul odors. Dust. Pollution. Pollen. Smoke. Carbon monoxide. The upright and reversed definitions are about the same.

8 OF CUPS: Walking away from a relationship or something one invested time, emotion, and energy in. Leaving everything behind (physically, emotionally or metaphorically). Putting it behind you. Abandoning a plan or project. Turning their back. Getting smooth away with it. Change of plans. Going in a new direction. Breaking new ground. Innovation. Exploring the unknown. Pioneering. Hiking. Emigrants (legal or illegal). Refugees. Evacuating. This card repeatedly came up for the mass evacuations of hurricane Katrina.

8 OF CUPS (Reversed): Not walking away. Deciding to stay. Staying even if it is hopeless and pointless, or no longer rewarding or beneficial. They are refusing to leave when you've asked them to go. Or, they won't go where you are wanting them to go. Wandering around lost. Having Alzheimer's.

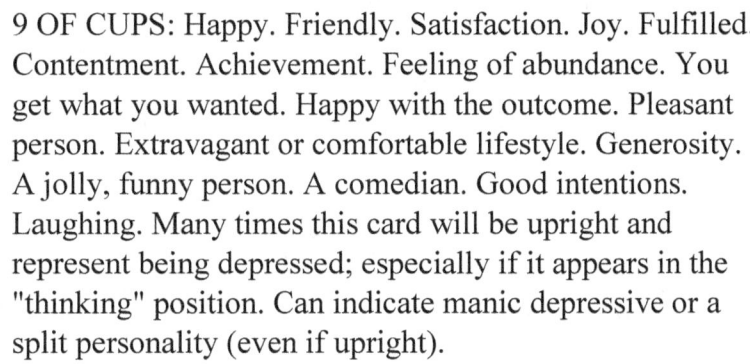

9 OF CUPS: Happy. Friendly. Satisfaction. Joy. Fulfilled. Contentment. Achievement. Feeling of abundance. You get what you wanted. Happy with the outcome. Pleasant person. Extravagant or comfortable lifestyle. Generosity. A jolly, funny person. A comedian. Good intentions. Laughing. Many times this card will be upright and represent being depressed; especially if it appears in the "thinking" position. Can indicate manic depressive or a split personality (even if upright).

9 OF CUPS (Reversed): Unhappy. Depressed. A person who is never satisfied and who is difficult or impossible to please. Emotionally unstable. Mood swings. Manic depressive. You will not get what you wished for. Their intentions are unfriendly. Does not like them. An unpleasant personality.

10 OF CUPS: Happy family. A family united in love and joy. A devoted family. Focus is on family and is important to them. An adopted family. A family reunion. Family increases. Starting a family. Can be any group that makes you feel loved or treated as part of the family. A large, extended family. Feeling fulfilled.

10 OF CUPS (Reversed): Problems with the family. Family members are quarreling. Disconnected from family. Ostracized from or kicked out of the family. Broken home due to divorce or death. Family has grown apart. They do not have a family. An orphan. Grew up in foster care. Feeling their family is not complete. Lost an important family member. Missing their family. Homesick.

PAGE OF CUPS: A child. A young person with artistic, intuitive and psychic abilities. The child is intelligent, gifted, and creative. A much beloved child. A favorite child. A good student. A child who brings joy. Any free spirited person no matter the age. Young at heart. Can represent a female child if question is of gender.

PAGE OF CUPS (Reversed): There is a problem with this child. Physically or mentally handicapped. Mental retardation. Mongoloid. Mentally incompetent. Crippled. An emotionally disturbed child. A worrisome child. The word 'disabled' in relation to person or to an object. The word 'unable'. Working with the disabled. A self-centered, childish person of any age.

KNIGHT OF CUPS: Romance. The arrival of a suitor. Wooing or being wooed. Declaration of love. Love offering. Dating. A marriage proposal. Offering or receiving a proposal or proposition. A good opportunity. In good faith. Benefiting. Prospecting. Having good potential. Someone who travels over the ocean and waters. A seafaring person. Flooding issues.

KNIGHT OF CUPS (Reversed): Cheating. Infidelity. An affair. Unfaithful lover. Taking their love elsewhere. Relationship based on deceit and lies. The romance is off. This person does not really care about you and will never make a commitment. An unrequited, unreturned love interest. Being suspicious of unfaithfulness, whether true or unfounded. To determine if they are truly cheating look for court cards that represent other people or the 7 of swords (be careful telling a seeker their love is cheating on them). No prospects, no offers, no opportunities. Medically: Edema, fluid overload. Pleurisy.

QUEEN OF CUPS: A water sign woman (Pisces, Scorpio, Cancer). Mother. Wife. A mother figure (any female relative). An affectionate woman. A beautiful woman. She is highly creative and artistic. She has psychic ability and insight. One's appearance. Beauty. Beautician. Cosmetics. The physical appearance of a thing or object. A light haired or light skinned woman.

QUEEN OF CUPS (Reversed): Troubles with their mother, wife, female relative, ex-wife or ex-girlfriend. A bad mother. No mothering skills. An argumentative wife. A cheating wife. A dishonest, untrustworthy woman. A gossiping woman. Being gossiped about. Being betrayed by a woman. The 'other' woman. They don't find her pretty or she feels unattractive for some reason. An item that is not in good cosmetic condition. Skin or other 'cosmetic' problems. Problem with one's appearance. Medically: Cosmetic issues. Acne. Boils. Scars. Skin cancer. Disfigured.

KING OF CUPS: Husband. Father. A father figure. Father in law. A water sign man (Pisces, Cancer, Scorpio). Doctor. A light haired or light skinned male. An emotional, sensitive, or tender-hearted male. Mentoring male who is supportive. The big-brother type.

KING OF CUPS (Reversed): Problem with husband or father. An ex-husband. Estranged husband. Husband has left the wife. Personality or character flaws in a man. A dishonest and untrustworthy male. Emotional betrayal. A rejection or neglect issue with their father, husband, or the father of the children. Either the seeker is the one being denied or rejected by this male figure, or they are doing the rejecting. A person who says one thing and does another. Makes promises but doesn't follow through.

Wands

ACE OF WANDS: Creation. Life. Birth. Fertility. Pregnant. Creativity. Brilliant or profitable idea. Inspired. Inventions. Lucrative business endeavors. Physical chemistry. Lots of Charisma. Thrilling. Exciting. They are alive. Dynamic. Attraction. Hormones. Enzymes. Electricity. Energy. Magnetic. Carries a charge. Nuclear power. Radiation. Laser. Multi media. Video. Biological or chemical organisms. DNA. Sperm. Ova. Genetics.

ACE OF WANDS (Reversed): We are biological, chemical and electrical organisms. Our bodies are run by hormones, chemicals, neurotransmitters. Problems with these processes are too numerous to list. Provided are just a few. Genetic problem or birth defects. Dead versus alive. Infertility. Neurological disorders. Seizures. Parkinson's. Fibromyalgia. Chronic fatigue. Multiple Sclerosis. Chemical imbalances in the brain. Manic Depressive. Depression. Hormone problems. PMS. Inflammatory processes. Sprains. Broken bone. Bone marrow problems (leukemia, neutropenia). Allergic reactions (anaphylaxis), immuno-suppressed. Bacteria & viruses (flu, SARS, small pox, hepatitis, herpes, molds, fungus, anthrax, Ebola, HIV). Bio-chemical organism (natural or man-made). Radiation or chemotherapy. Antibiotics (against life). Electrical problems. Radioactive. Shocked or electrocuted. Fire. Explosion. Fireworks. Hot. Burn. Gun-shot or bullet.

2 OF WANDS: Self-esteem and confidence. Having goals. Strong, healthy ego. A capable person who is ready to move forward in life and is surveying their prospects. Prospects look good. They are ambitious and building upon past successes. Having a good outlook on life. The "world is their oyster". They can pursue anything they please. Someone or something is good for their ego and self-esteem. Anticipation. Watching and waiting for something. Awaiting a response from someone.

2 OF WANDS (Reversed): Poor self-esteem and lack of confidence. They have no goals. They have no idea what they want to do with their life. No

successes to build upon. Not advancing or progressing. Not being assertive. Not a go-getter. Having insecurities. Under-estimating ones abilities. Feeling incapable. Settling for less. The prospects are poor. Someone or something is damaging their ego and self-esteem. Sudden loss of self-confidence due to a precipitating event. An issue of ego (too much or too little).

3 OF WANDS: Business success. Successful merchant. Business owner. Entrepreneur. Networking. Expanding. New prospects or business relations. Importing & exporting. Wealth through international exchange. Looking to join up with (such as marines, or armed forces). Oil rich countries (oil=liquid gold). Off shore oil drilling (came up for British Petroleum spill). Fracking.

3 OF WANDS (Reversed): Business problems. Business is slowed. Poor prospects. Going out of business, willingly or unwillingly. The business is down or has failed. Warning that it is not a good business venture. The company is not sound. Trouble with oil countries or oil companies.

4 OF WANDS: Marriage. A wedding. Romance. Building a life together as a couple. Living together as if married. Establishing a firm foundation in any relationship, including friendships. Providing a solid foundation for another, including children. Sharing your life with another (of any age or relation). Can refer to the foundation or structure of a home or building. Being on solid ground with an issue or person.

4 OF WANDS (Reversed): A relationship (legally married or not) that is over or is not working. Wanting out of the marriage. Divorced. One party refuses to marry the other. Never been married. An unfaithful marriage. Not having a strong foundation to the endeavor or relationship; nothing to build upon. Problems with the foundation, roof, or structure when asking about a house or building. For example, this card with the 5 of pentacles would indicate structural problems because the foundation is "sick" or "injured".

5 OF WANDS: Mental anxiety. Mental conflicts. Obstacles. Strife. Struggle. Competition. Rivalry. Indecision. Excessive mental activity. Trying to mentally solve a problem. Over thinking. Worrying. General anxiety disorder. Post-traumatic stress disorder.

5 OF WANDS (Reversed): Not worrying anymore. They aren't worried about it. Not giving any thought to it.

6 OF WANDS: Honor and appreciation. Admiration. Public acclamation. Public vindication. Honored. Someone famous. Celebrity. A public figure. Admired and well respected. Being well received. A returning hero. Recognized in their field. Reaching goals. A good reputation. Triumph. Victory.

6 OF WANDS (Reversed): Not being, or just not feeling appreciated. Not being acknowledged. Being, or just feeling disrespected and dishonored. A plan or action did not succeed. Defamation of character. Having a bad reputation. Receiving a negative referral or reference. Their background check is bad.

7 OF WANDS: Success. Winning. Overcoming obstacles. Coming out on top. Holding one's ground. Taking a stand. Having the upper hand or advantage. Facing the opposition. Accepting the challenge. You will succeed.

7 OF WANDS (Reversed): Unsuccessful. Failing. Won't win. Will not challenge. They quit or want to quit. Gave up. Surrendering. Easily influenced or easily swayed. Being over ruled or outnumbered. Obstacles are too great and cannot be overcome. Insurmountable. This is a losing battle.

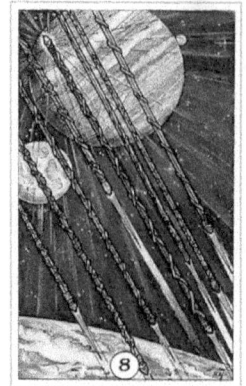

8 OF WANDS: Advancement. Expanding. Prospering. Growth happening. Job promotion. Rapid action or motion. Movement. Activity. Taking action. Projectile. Missiles. Sudden attack. Speeding. Fast. Quickly. Done hastily. Going far (physically or metaphorically). Indicates time. Gaining more time. A long time. A timeline. Spanning several generations. Outer space. Planets. Comets. Meteorites. Observatory. Astronomy. Astrology. Space program. The space shuttle.

8 OF WANDS (Reversed): No advancement happening. Delays and stagnation. Losing ground. Going backwards. Overdue. On hold. Boredom. Period of inaction. Not happening fast enough. Too slow. Too fast. Lack of time. Not the right time to take action. Bad timing. Speed causes a problem. Physical exhaustion. Burnout. Stimulants. Amphetamines. Caffeine.

9 OF WANDS: On the defensive. Taking a stand. Defending oneself or another. Willing to do battle. Won't back down. Determined. Prepared to fight. Guarding. Being on guard. Security guard. Anticipating struggles. Encountering obstacles. Facing difficulties. Maintaining their position. Defiance. A struggle. A martial artist (Karate). Skilled in art of self-defense. Survivalist. Prepper.

9 OF WANDS (Reversed): They quit, gave up. Losing the battle. Cut your losses and get out. Whatever it was, it is over. Releasing the need to struggle. Refusing to face the challenge. Doesn't like confrontation. Won't confront them. Unequipped. Does not possess the skill to face the challenge. Easily over-whelmed by obstacles. Unable to defend one's position. Defenseless. No backbone. Lacks willpower and determination.

10 OF WANDS: A hard worker. Doing their duty. All work, no play. Taking on the responsibility. Taking on more than you can handle. Over-worked. Keeping their nose to the grindstone. Working on their feet or carrying heavy loads. Carrying the guilt (weight on their shoulders). They are a carrier, courier, or deliver things. Carried on their person. Walking, hiking, jogging. Medical: Hip, back or knee problems making it difficult to walk.

10 OF WANDS (Reversed): Burden lifted. Refusing to support themselves. Being dependent on others. Letting others carry their load. Laziness. Being irresponsible. Medically: Difficulty walking. Walking stooped over. Hunch back. Walks with a limp. Back, hip or knee problems. Uses walker, cane, or special shoes. Osteoarthritis. Weight issues (too heavy or too thin).

PAGE OF WANDS: Giving or receiving a message. Invitation. Speaking. Calling. Talking. Yelling. Talking about it or hearing about it. Broadcasting it. Sounding an alarm. Making a noise of any kind. Marriage proposal. All forms of communication and media. All jobs that involve communication. Electronics. Video. Multimedia. Computers. Internet. Twitter. Skype. Youtube. Email. Texting. Faxing. Making a purchase. Buying. Selling. Public speaker. Seminar. Publishing. Electronic transfer of data. Reporters. Newspapers. Radio. Commercials. Marketing. Advertisement. Stock market. Broadcasting. Our communication senses (seeing, hearing, smelling, speaking).

PAGE OF WANDS (Reversed): Communication problems. Did not like what was communicated. Saying the wrong thing. An information problem or breakdown, whether in delivery or understanding. They cannot or will not communicate with you. Won't answer the phone, email, or texts. Having a problem with the language. Unable to use the equipment, or a problem with the equipment. Problems with multimedia, computers, the internet, the stock market, publishing, or advertisements. Problem with a purchase. Problems with buying or selling. All the reverse of the upright position. Medically: trouble hearing, seeing, or speaking. Laryngitis. Deafness. Mute. Aphasia.

KNIGHT OF WANDS: Traveling. Taking a trip. Moving. Changing residence. Taking action. Motivation. Quick, energetic, enthusiastic, or urgent action. Enthusiasm for taking an action. Traveling or driving as a career. Transportation. Truck or taxi driver. A moving company. Tow trucks. Delivery trucks. UPS. Being taken to jail (which is a change of residence or forced action). Read literally, horses or large animals. Having a muscular build.

KNIGHT OF WANDS (Reversed): Forced to change their residence. Thrown out of the house. Eviction. Forced to move where they don't want to move, including going to jail. Wishing they could move. Having to move out of necessity. Unable to take action. Slow to action, or not taking action. Forced into taking action. A trip is delayed or canceled. Problem with horses or large animals. Medically: muscular or neuromuscular disorders. Multiple sclerosis. Tremors. Parkinson's. Fibromyalgia. Gillian Barre. Muscular Dystrophy. Myasthenia Gravis. Muscle cramps.

QUEEN OF WANDS: Fire sign female (Aries, Leo, Sagittarius). A woman with stage presence. A speaker. A singer. Socially prominent. Actress. Performer. A 'social light'. Flair for drama. Likes being the center of attention and 'center-stage'. She is energetic, passionate, action oriented. A woman of any sign who has outgoing and energetic qualities. Blond or red haired woman.

QUEEN OF WANDS (Reversed): Socially withdrawn. Extremely shy. Anti-social. Isolated from others. Having an inhibited and reserved personality. They refuse to talk to someone, or someone is not talking to them. An alternative interpretation could be that this woman is jealous or vengeful. This person could be of any sign and have these positive or negative qualities.

 KING OF WANDS: Fire sign male (Aries, Leo, Sagittarius). An assertive, energetic, enthusiastic, passionate male. Charismatic. Salesman. Entertainer. Musician. Stage or public personality. Famous and well known. Very sociable and enjoys being the center of attention. A blond or red haired man. American Indian. A gay male.

KING OF WANDS (Reversed): A man with all the negative characteristics of the upright King of Wands. Loud and obnoxious. Obstinate behavior. Disgusting and obscene. Hostile. Belligerent. Combative. An assaulter. A man who is clinging to a female in a jealous fashion. An ex husband or ex boyfriend.

Pentacles

ACE OF PENTACLES: Financial success and security. A successful business venture. Large investment. Those who handle a lot of money. A stock or bond. Capital gains. Startup capital. Receiving a sum of money. Something is expensive. Huge expenses. The physical, manifested realm. The earth. The physical body. Can represent anything physical, such as equipment.

ACE OF PENTACLES (Reversed): Great loss of money. Financial ruin. Bankruptcy. Large amount of money spent. A large down payment. Large debt or payment owed. Maxed out the credit cards. Heavy loss in the stock market. Poverty. Could just represent fears about being broke if in the thinking position. The soul is earthbound (in questions about a departed loved one). Broken equipment. Equipment failure. A thing or person being in poor physical condition. Physical assault and battery.

2 OF PENTACLES: Balanced. Stable. Capable. Multitasking. Good technique. Performing well under pressure. A 'balancing act'. Weighing a dilemma. Deliberating on the pros and cons of a matter, or two equally attractive prospects in order to make a choice. Prospecting. Forming an opinion. Things are "still up in the air". Two of a thing. An exchange or transfer. Mixing or combining things. Switching of two things. It is cyclic. A thing spinning. Tornado. El' Nino. Hurricane. A cable or phone company. Wiring or transferring money. Cables or wires. Wheels. Medically: the legs, feet and ankles. Having a fall. Hurting a leg, foot, or ankle (same for reversed card). This card kept coming up for hurricane Katrina (plus 8 cups for evacuations).

2 OF PENTACLES (Reversed): Falling. Tripping. Breaking, spraining, or hurting a leg, foot, or ankle. Problems with leg or foot area. Needing shoes, special shoes or wheel chair. Thrown off balance. Vertigo. Loss of equilibrium. Unable to juggle demands. Overwhelmed. Not able to formulate an opinion or make a choice. Two items are unequal, not the same in some way. Not having the same value as the other. It's a 'bait and switch'. Too

much of one thing compared to another. A thing out of balance. Problems with phone, cable company, or electrical wiring. Problem wiring money.

3 OF PENTACLES: A job. Getting a new job. An increase in rank, duty, prestige and earnings. A master craftsman. Skilled in a profession or trade. A trained craft. Having marketable skills. Intricate detailed work. Sculpting. Chiseling. Carving. Building something. Indicates it is manmade. Creating something of enduring and lasting beauty. Working on something, like a project.

3 OF PENTACLES (Reversed): Lost their job. Laid off. No pleasure in their work, or not being able to work. Stuck in a job they don't like. No marketable skills. Not skilled at their current job. Unskilled labor. Poor workmanship. They have no job. Resigning. They don't want to work. Work alcoholic versus lazy. Problems with a project.

4 OF PENTACLES: Possessive. Greedy. Selfish. Envy. Clinging. Won't share. Mistrustful. Afraid someone is going to take it away. Unable to let go of a thing tangible or intangible. They want it back. Hanging on in a stubborn way. They, like, really - really want it. Hoarding. Squirreling it away. In their possession. Keeping it private. Being protective. Tucking something or <u>someone</u> away for safe-keeping. Hidden from prying eyes. protecting one's privacy. Keeping it private. Securing it. A safe. Guarding what they have. Wants others to stay away. Hiding out. A hideout. A storm shelter.

4 OF PENTACLES (Reversed): Releasing. Letting it go. Forgiving and forgetting. Forgiveness. The message is to let it go (physically or metaphorically). They do not hold it as being dear to them. There are no safeguards or protections being provided or awarded to it. A thing or person is not being kept safe. Medical: problem in arms, wrists, or hands. Arthritis.

5 OF PENTACLES: Illness. Injury. Disease. Sick. Being in poor health. Declining health. Aging. Physical deterioration. Poverty. Being poor. Impoverished. Having a feeling of being poor. Feeling or being destitute. Suffering. Hardships. Outcast. Feeling rejected. Mistreated. Suffering violence. Physical abuse. Neglected. Abandoned. Beggar. Homeless. Medical: all illnesses or injury. Amputations.

5 OF PENTACLES (Reversed): Health restored. Reversal of poverty. Health issue correctable or in the process of correcting. Illness in remission. Healing taking place. They will recover. Works with the handicapped, injured, or abused (up right or reversed).

6 OF PENTACLES: Financial stability. Paying all the bills, debts and creditors. Making ends meet with something left over. They owe a lot of people. Sharing. Charity. Donating. Helping the less fortunate in times of need. Giving or receiving assistance; usually involves financial aid given but can be any help rendered. Humanitarian aid. On financial aid.

6 OF PENTACLES (Reversed): Not making ends meet. Unable to pay all the bills. Too many bills and creditors. Financially unstable. Over drawn. Over-extended. Bounced checks. Unable to support themselves. Not receiving the assistance they needed or expected. Wanting to help but not able to. No giving or receiving is going on.

7 OF PENTACLES: Work. Getting a new job. Menial or manual labor. Handyman. Farmer. Gardener. Gardening. Landscaping. Plants. Construction worker. Loves the outdoors. Woodsman. A hunter. Time to reap the rewards from their labor. A plan that comes to fruition. Harvest time. Satisfaction from a job well done. This card is interchangeable with 3 of pentacles for job or work. The message, "In due time". Could be read as a period of 7 months (or sometime within the next 7 months).

7 OF PENTACLES (Reversed): Lost or quit the job. Looking for work. Don't like or want the job. Unable to reap the harvest of their hard work. Long laid plans are dashed. There is no future potential in the project. Disappointment or failure in some enterprise.

8 OF PENTACLES: Training. Studying. School. Classroom. Reading. Writing. Signature. Autograph. Reports. Paper work. Books. Documents. Notarized. Clerical. Contract. Records. Journal. Diary. Email. Letter. A writer. A teacher. A student. Studious child. Learning a new skill or knowledge. Learning the tools of the trade. Apprenticeship. Craftsmanship. Working with wood, cabinetmaking, wood carvings. Assembling. Concentrating on the work at hand. Planning. They planned it.

8 OF PENTACLES (Reversed): Untrained. Uneducated. Illiterate. Drop-out. Failing. Skipped school. Reading or learning disability. Lied about their training or education. Didn't do their homework. Didn't do their due diligence. Didn't read it. Problem with a document or contract. Undocumented illegal immigrant. Dread signing papers (divorce, etc.').

9 OF PENTACLES: Affluent. Wealthy. Financially secure. Above average income. Feeling secure and self-confident. Material comforts. Pampered, sheltered life. Well dressed. Elegance. One's personal and material possessions. Unscathed by turmoil's affecting others. Luxury items (jewelry, cloths, furniture). Actual garden or flowers. Outdoors. Outside. Land. Acreage. A secured environment, boundary, area, or compound. FEMA camps. A shelter. A "safe house" or safe haven.

9 OF PENTACLES (Reversed): Loss of wealth or personal property. Loss of financial independence, possibly having to rely on another for financial support. Bad financial planning. Having lost 'the farm'. Bankruptcy. Feelings of insecurity or a lack of confidence. This is not a safe or secure environment. Border or compound is not secure.

10 OF PENTACLES: Home. House. Apartment. Office. Hotel room. A room. Any building. In the house. Homemaker. Focus is on home and family. Time off to stay home. Home bound. A peaceful and tranquil home and family life. Planning to purchase a home. Renovations or home improvements. In the business of home construction, home repairs, real estate, or investor.

10 OF PENTACLES (Reversed): Disruptive or unhappy home life. Too many people in the house. Evicted or thrown out. Having no place to live. Lost the house. Foreclosure. Afraid to leave the house (agoraphobia). Homebound. Grounded. Structural problems (roof leaks, foundation cracked, appliances broke). Living in the projects. Fights over who gets the house. You don't get the house.

PAGE OF PENTACLES: Payments, dues, and fees. Gifts. Child support. Money or gifts to a child. An allowance. Paying for school, classes, private school or college. A grant or scholarship. A bonus check. Sharing. An item of value. Payments made in installments (on layaway). Payback is now due. Making restitution. The 8 rays can indicate portions, parts or portions of a whole, or fractions of a whole or indicate blocks of time. 6 months. Ethnic child. A non-biological child.

PAGE OF PENTACLES (Reversed): Not sharing or giving a portion. Not giving a gift. No money for school supplies or education. No grants, loans, or scholarship. No money to the kids. Unable to support the child's expenses. No child support. Not receiving a gift. Lost money (purse, wallet, credit card, etc.'). Nonpayment (credit cards, rent, fees). Unable to buy or purchase an item. The step-child. Rejects the child. Can mean, "because it is not their child." A lazy, non-productive child. Parts of a whole but not the whole. Parts missing. Partially. Part time.

KNIGHT OF PENTACLES: Getting a bank loan. Getting credit cards. Getting checks or other payments. Getting a nice sum of money. Someone of a reliable nature who helps them in any way. Making good money. Receiving or giving personal or financial assistance to others.

KNIGHT OF PENTACLES (Reversed): Not getting the loan. Not getting the financial help they need. They do not support you. Problems with money. An unreliable person, probably uninterested in employment. They are not financially dependable. Lost significant amount of money. Bad credit reports. Lost the credit card or lost the checks.

QUEEN OF PENTACLES: Earth-sign woman (Virgo, Capricorn, Taurus). Handles money or loans. Works for a bank or in a loan department. Good business practices. Efficient and dependable woman. A practical and 'down to earth' woman; not necessarily an earth sign. An ethnic woman with dark hair and skin. Things that are "earthy," meaning dirt, fruits and vegetables.

** This card consistently came up for the smoldering and burning peat-moss of the Russian fires in July 2010. Pentacles are the physical realm and Queen of Pentacles is "earth-woman" and hence represents products of 'mother-earth'. It is interesting that the nickname for Russia is the 'Mother-Land'. Other cards were 7 Cups + 8 Cups for smoke and evacuations.

QUEEN OF PENTACLES (Reversed): Woman of reduced means. She is broke. Being impractical in business. A woman financially dependent on others. Handles money poorly. She might manage money appropriately but be in a temporary position where money is tight.

KING OF PENTACLES: Earth sign male (Virgo, Capricorn, Taurus). Wealthy. A rich man or woman. Old money. Financially established person. A large savings (nest egg). Comfortable retirement. 401k's. Retirement funds. A corporate head who manages the money. Financial institutions. Banks. Stock markets. Bank rolling a project. A reliable man that you can financially count on.

KING OF PENTACLES (Reversed): A huge financial loss. Loss of savings or retirement money. Keep an eye on your accounts and take precautions. No financial means or backing. Heavily in debt. Financial stress. A financial institution that is in trouble. Shady business practices. Dishonest businessman. He will take you for your money. Scrutinize all business contracts and negotiations. Squanders the money away. Medically: Liver problems (the liver is the master organ).

Medical Assignments

Some cards have a medical issue assigned to them. You can also assign your own if you like. Just remember that you cannot diagnose or give medical advice without a medical license. At the same time, if used judicially, you just might save a life.

3 Empress ~ Pregnancy. Abdominal issues, which includes stomach, uterus and ovaries or the breasts, gallbladder, pancreas.

6 Lovers ~ Reproductive organs, which includes private areas. For men, it is prostate issues. Also indicates all transmittable diseases and infections from person to person and not just those that are sexually transmitted (example: MRSA).

8 Strength ~ Allergies. Asthma. Bacteria. Parasites. Worms. Fleas. Mites. Yeast infection. Anxiety disorders. Panic attacks. Chronic fatigue.

9 Hermit ~ Vision problems. Cataracts. Blind. Elderly. Any person or object that is old (ex: old food, old clothes, old car, old house). Decrepit. Senior.

11 Justice ~ Medical tests and diagnostics.

12 Hanged Man ~ Head and neck areas. Choked. Drowned. Hanged. Beheaded. Suffocated. Strangled. A disincarnate entity. A spirit attachment or influence. Snake, spider, scorpion, or other biting and stinging insects.

13 Death ~ Chronic condition. Menopause. In a dormant state. In remission.

14 Temperance ~ Stress. Burn out. Metals in the body (lead, aluminum).

15 Devil ~ Addictions. Toxins. Poison. Rotten. Pollutants. Drugs.

18 Moon ~ Mental aberrations and illness. Confusion. ADHD. Schizophrenia. Bipolar. Stroke. Coma. Unconscious. Amnesia. Dementia. Alzheimer's. Hallucinations. Sun Downers (elderly who get more confused-agitated at night). Cysts. Growths. Tumors.

19 Sun ~ Overheated. Sun Stroke. Sun burned. Depression. Seasonal Affective Disorder (SAD), which just means they need to get more sun.

20 Judgement ~ If upright it means full recovery and good health. Exercise. Physically fit. Acupuncture. Chiropractor. Physical therapy. The naked body. If reversed, means poor health, doesn't recover, a thing is not purified or cleansed, immune system down, feeling drained of their energy. Slow metabolism.

21 World ~ Circulation. Metastasized. Blood pressure problems.

Ace Pentacles ~ Physical abuse.

2 Pentacles ~ Tripping. Falling. Problem with leg, feet, ankles. Sprains.

4 Pentacle ~ Arthritis. Problems with hands, arms, elbows.

5 Pentacles ~ Illness. Poverty. Abuse. Abandoned. Neglect.

King Pentacles ~ The boss organ, which is the Liver. Cirrhosis. Hepatitis C. Liver Cancer. Pancreatic cancer or pancreatitis.

Ace of Cups ~ Pregnancy. Fluid overload. Congested heart failure (CHF).

2 Cups ~ Kidney problems.

3 Cups ~ Diabetic. Alcoholic. Food allergies. Malnutrition. Anorexia. Bulimia.

5 Cups ~ Blood loss. Anemia. Grief.

7 Cups ~ Smoke. Dust. Ash. Fumes. Odors. Heavy smoker. Carbon monoxide. Pollen. Pollution. Suffocation. Nightmares. Also, asthma.

9 Cups ~ Unhappy. Bipolar. Emotionally unstable. Mood swings. Manic depressive. Goofy person.

Page Cups ~ Disabled, mentally or physically handicapped, mongoloid.

Knight Cups ~ Edema. Congestion.

Queen Cups ~ Cosmetic issues. Disfigured. Boils, warts, scars, acne, skin cancer.

King Cups ~ Doctor.

Ace Swords ~ Sharp pain. Needle stick. Shots. IV drug usage. IV therapy.

3 Swords ~ Accident or injury. Sudden illness. Death. Cut. Stabbed. Shot. Punctured. Ruptured. Surgery. Heart attack surgery. Pierces. Stroke. Tattoos.

4 Swords ~ Rest and relaxation. Bed rest. Sleep problems.

7 Swords ~ Crime being committed against them. Homicidal.

8 Swords ~ Lung or rib problems. Can't move.

9 Swords ~ Emotional or physical pain. Fibromyalgia.

10 Swords ~ Spinal problems. Broken back. Blood disorders. Ruptured Spleen. Metal plates or pins. Prosthetics. Exhaustion. Depleted.

Knight Swords ~ Cancer. Anger issues.

Queen Swords ~ Nurse. Clinic. Hospital. Healer. Veterinarian.

King Swords ~ Surgeon (king cups = doctor)

Ace Wands ~ Pregnancy. Birth. Fertility. DNA. Sperm or Ova. Genetics. <u>Negative aspects:</u> Birth defects. Genetic or neurological disorders. Seizures. Fibromyalgia. Multiple Sclerosis. Chemical imbalances. Manic Depressive. Hormones. PMS. Sprains. Strains. Broken bone. Neutropenia. Leukemia, Allergies. Immuno-suppressed. Bacteria & viruses (flu, small pox, hepatitis, herpes, molds, fungus, AIDS). Chemotherapy. Radiation. Antibiotics. Shocked or electrocuted. Burned. Inflammation. Impotency. Low libido.

5 Wands ~ Worry. Anxiety. Over thinking a thing.

10 Wands ~ Difficulty walking. Walking stooped over. Hunch back. Walks with a limp. Back, hip or knee problems. Uses walker, cane, or special shoes. Osteoarthritis. Weight issues. They are a "carrier" of this disease.

Page Wands ~ Problems with speech or hearing. Receptive or expressive problems. Aphasia. Laryngitis. Deaf or mute.

Knight Wands ~ Muscle and neuromuscular issues. Tremors. Parkinson's. Muscle cramps. Multiple Sclerosis. Gillian Barre. Muscular Dystrophy. Myasthenia Gravis. ALS or Lou Gehrig's Disease.

Bonus

The 22 Major cards of Tarot (0 thru 21) represent the 7 planets of Mars, Venus, Mercury, Jupiter, Neptune, Saturn, and Uranus. Plus, the sun, moon, and star, which makes 10. Plus, the 12 constellations of Aries, Taurus, Gemini, Cancer, Leo, Virgo, Libra, Scorpio, Sagittarius, Capricorn, Aquarius, and Pisces. These are my assignments based upon my own research. Others may not agree.

The ancients used a symbol called the Tau cross in the form of an X to represent the 4 "fixed" constellations. They were considered "fixed" because they did not appear to move (from earth's perspective). These four points are marked by Taurus (ox), Leo (lion), Scorpio (Aquila, an eagle), and Aquarius (divine man). They are the 4 faces of the living creature of Revelations said to be before the throne of God.

The cards I have assigned to the Tau X are the Star card for Taurus (the Pleiades constellation), the Strength card for Leo (the lion), the Judgement card for Scorpio (Aquila the Eagle) and Temperance card for Aquarius (the divine man).

The symbol of a cross + (used long before Christianity) marks the 4 seasons. The right and left points mark the spring and fall equinoxes of Aries (lamb) and Libra (scales). The north and south points mark the summer solstice in Cancer (crab) and winter solstice in Capricorn (goat). These points also mark the four directions of north, south, east, and west and the four elements of earth (carbon), air (nitrogen), fire (oxygen), and water (hydrogen). Also of the principles of spiritual, psychic, mental, and physical. And also the four humors of melancholic, choleric, sanguine, and phlegmatic.

The cards I assigned to the points of the Cross + are Magician (Hermes) for Aries. From Hermes we get the Hermetic wisdom teachings. He was considered the messenger of God. His is often imaged with a lamb. The bible and Qabalah are rooted in Hermetic Science. Then, Hermit (Hermetic) for Cancer (standing at the north pole keeping the sacred science of the precession of the equinox.). The Justice card is Libra (scales) and the Devil card is Capricorn (goat).

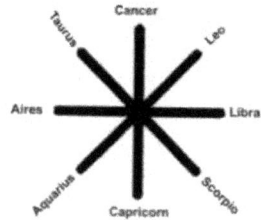

Together (Tau and Cross) make the 8 pointed star of the goddess Ishtar associated with the planet Venus, whose principle "house of beauty" is Taurus, and so Venus becomes, "the Star of Taurus". So, even though Taurus is an ox/bull, in this constellation is the all-important 7 sister stars of the Pleiades.

In the background is the High Priestess. She holds the Torah of the ancient mystery teachings. She is the infinite, blue watery oceans of the heavens. In physics, she is the ethers (aethers) that fills all space. In theology, she is Shekinah and Sophia of God's Wisdom. ✷

1

10 of Cups, 13, 27, 31, 41, 88
10 of Pentacles, 19, 21, 23, 36, 53, 102
10 of Swords, 15, 22, 59, 81, 107
10 of Wands, 21, 25, 29, 41, 95, 107

2

2 of Cups., 27, 31, 33, 35, 47, 84, 106
2 of Pentacles, 16, 17, 35, 55, 98, 106
2 of Swords, 11, 25, 41, 51, 59, 77
2 of Wands, 19, 33, 60, 91

3

3 of Cups, 9, 21, 31, 55, 58, 61, 85,106
3 of Pentacles, 12, 30, 51, 57, 99
3 of Swords, 23, 27, 30, 48, 55, 71, 78, 106
3 of Wands, 30, 46, 92

4

4 of Cups, 8, 10, 21, 51, 55, 63, 85, 106
4 of Pentacles, 19, 23, 29, 35, 41, 58, 99, 106
4 of Swords, 13, 15, 21, 28, 34, 37, 43, 57, 79, 106
4 of Wands, 18, 24, 32, 59, 63, 92

5

5 of Cups, 13, 15, 27, 49, 85
5 of Pentacles, 13, 14, 29, 35, 41, 45, 55, 100, 106
5 of Swords, 9, 17, 19, 23, 41, 47, 48, 59, 79
5 of Wands, 8, 15, 48, 93, 107

6

6 of Cups, 6, 15, 51, 53, 86, 106
6 of Pentacles, 9, 10, 31, 37, 38, 43, 100
6 of Swords, 7, 11, 19, 27, 55, 79
6 of Wands, 9, 29, 57, 60, 93

7

7 of Cups, 11, 17, 21, 22, 25, 47, 84, 104, 106
7 of Pentacles, 8, 31, 54, 101
7 of Swords, 9, 19, 23, 27, 35, 39, 41, 49, 55, 59, 76, 80, 106
7 of Wands, 17, 35, 37, 46, 59, 93

8

8 of Cups, 17, 23, 39, 47, 53, 87, 104
8 of Pentacles, 7, 33, 43, 45, 47, 101
8 of Swords, 17, 23, 39, 52, 57, 80, 107
8 of Wands, 7, 9, 33, 43, 45, 51, 56, 62, 94

9

9 of Cups, 7, 19, 21, 27, 31, 35, 59, 87, 106
9 of Pentacles, 19, 41, 53, 102
9 of Swords, 15, 19, 28, 39, 41, 53, 81, 107
9 of Wands, 7, 11, 24, 35, 48, 55, 61, 94

A

Ace of Cups, 24, 39, 47, 50, 67, 73, 84, 98, 106
Ace of Pentacles, 7, 20, 38, 40, 43, 53, 64, 71, 98, 112, 106
Ace of Swords, 20 24, 28, 45, 55, 60, 67, 71, 77, 90, 106
Ace of Wands, 28, 34, 35, 42, 43, 50, 52, 58, 64, 72, 91, 107

B

Blank Card, 89

C

Chariot, 9, 13, 23, 44, 52, 54, 55, 68

D

Death, 8, 23, 55, 71, 78, 81, 86, 88, 71, 78, 105
Devil, 19, 23, 24, 39, 45, 51, 55, 72, 105

E

Emperor, 18, 49, 59, 61, 67
Empress, 6, 14, 28, 41, 66, 105

F

Fool, 10, 25, 29, 37, 39, 43, 50, 55, 65, 75

H

Hanged Man, 16, 18, 31, 32, 43, 51, 55, 71, 105
Hermit, 6, 8, 12, 26, 37, 39, 43, 47, 53, 55, 56, 61, 63, 69, 105
Hierophant, 13, 27, 42, 51, 57, 67, 73
High Priestess, 9, 42, 45, 52, 66

J

Judgement, 15, 29, 37, 54, 61, 75, 105
Justice, 6, 16, 31, 33, 39, 49, 55, 70, 105

K

King of Cups, 11, 25, 29, 90, 106
King of Pentacles, 19, 34, 39, 104
King of Swords, 7, 10, 18, 19, 20, 55, 83, 107
King of Wands, 27, 34, 97
Knight of Cups, 17, 62, 76, 89, 106
Knight of Pentacles, 37, 103, 106
Knight of Swords, 13, 14, 22, 23, 27, 37, 39, 41, 49, 53, 55, 80, 82, 107
Knight of Wands, 39, 96, 107

L

Lovers, 10, 11, 25, 26, 63, 68, 76, 105

M

Magician, 43, 45, 54, 65, 66
Moon, 20, 25, 57, 74, 105

P

Page of Cups, 11, 35, 88, 106
Page of Pentacles, 31, 61, 103
Page of Swords, 7, 11, 15, 22, 61, 81
Page of Wands, 19, 21, 23, 27, 31, 33, 45, 47, 48, 58, 63, 95, 107

Q

Queen of Cups, 20, 25, 38, 41, 53, 64, 89, 106
Queen of Pentacles, 23, 47, 64, 104
Queen of Swords, 14, 52, 64, 82, 107
Queen of Wands, 13, 26, 64, 96

S

Star, 19, 43, 73
Strength, 17, 33, 53, 54, 57, 69, 105
Sun, 28, 62, 63, 74, 105

T

Temperance, 32, 33, 37, 45, 51, 61, 72, 105
Tower, 13, 23, 45, 48, 59, 73, 78

W

Wheel of Fortune, 6, 28, 45, 61, 70
World, 11, 15, 46, 59, 63, 75, 106

www.ingramcontent.com/pod-product-compliance
Lightning Source LLC
Chambersburg PA
CBHW081459040426
42446CB00016B/3309